RACING AGAINST TIME

On Ironman, Ultramarathons, and the Quest for Transformation in Mid-Life

JEFFREY WEISS

Copyright 2025 by MSI Press LLC

All rights reserved. No part of this book may be reproduced or utilized in any form or by any means, electronic or mechanical, including photocopying and recording, or by any information storage and retrieval system without permission in writing from the publisher.

For information, contact
MSI Press, LLC
1760-F Airline Hwy #203
Hollister, CA 95023

Copyeditor: Betty Lou Leaver
Cover design & layout: Opeyemi Ikuborije
Photographs provided by the author

Living persons identified in this book have given permission for inclusion.

ISBN: 978-1-957354-69-9
Library of Congress Control Number: 2025910238

Dedication

*For Danny, Abby, Tali and Aaron for whom,
indeed, anything is possible.*

*For Orlie, whose love and support throughout so
many of the events described in this book meant
more to me than I can ever fully express.*

CONTENTS

Acknowledgments i

Prologue v

Free T-Shirt 1

Fast Forward 7

What Next 11

Triathlon 15

Speed, Sort Of 23

Marine Corps 27

The Magic of Two 39

Olympic Distance 49

End of the Line 53

A Message from Katherine Switzer 57

The Road to Comrades 65

The BHAG 71

No Turning Back 75

Going Beyond 26.2 79

The Spirit of Comrades 85

Shosholoza 91

Cut-Offs 99

Craziest Fucking Thing 109

Atlantic City 115

Bear Mountain 121

Regrouping	125
Cold Shock	127
Buoy to Buoy	133
You Are an Ironman	149
Return to Africa?	155
I Love LA	159
Best-Laid Plans	165
Lindsey Parry	169
The Iceman	179
Return to Arizona	183
Personally Victimized	189
And He's an Old Guy	197
Who is Going to Beat You Up?	201
The Sun Is Following You	207
San Francisco	213
The Why	219
The Return	225
Passing the Baton	237
What Next?	247
Missing the Crazy	253
Sorting Things Out	259
Escape from Burning Man	269
Midnight Express	281
41 Down/31 to Go	287
Find Your Ironman . . . And Your Comrades	295
References	301

Acknowledgments

Endurance sports, at least the way that I have pursued them, are a mostly solitary enterprise. I almost always train and compete by myself, spending long and challenging hours in the company of my own thoughts. And yet even for me, it has not been a lonely journey.

There are so many people who have helped me over the years. Lisa Levin and Julie Sapper, the coaches for the running class before my first 10K, taught me the running basics and got me properly launched. And a few years later Lisa coached me through my exhilarating 2012 Marine Corps Marathon.

As I became more serious about running, I had several friends whom I could always pepper with questions and who were always up for exchanging running stories. At the top of this list was Jason Schwartz, who first planted the running idea in my head when he shared his own remarkable story and who later played such a key role in getting me through Midnight Express. Greg and Jordana Ashe are both highly accomplished runners who have each qualified multiple times to run the Boston Marathon, and they were always a source of great insights and practical advice. Amy Subar, a former age group world champion in the Olympic distance triathlon, helped me make more sensible decisions when it came to triathlons. Amy also inspired me to write detailed post-race reports after each significant event, something that came in handy when I needed to revisit many of those during the writing of this book.

I have benefited tremendously from the assistance provided by the professional coaches that I have worked with over the years, including Lisa Levin, Don Fink, and the one-of-a-kind Lindsey Parry. Working with a coach has forced me, in nearly every single workout, to work harder and longer than I would have if I only had myself to answer to. In the process, they have gotten me to heights that I never could have reached on my own. Subsequent to the completion of this book, my fitness adventures have continued, with Lindsey still being the one who keeps me on track.

Orlie Braha was a constant source of support and encouragement—never a rolled eye or frustrated or cross word despite all the demands my training and racing schedule placed on my time. I will never forget her hidden notes during my first Ironman and her remarkable poster (now emblazoned with Mike Riley's autograph) at the finish line. Stories are legion of the toll that the extreme endurance lifestyle can take on a relationship but, thanks to Orlie, all the fitness craziness never drove a wedge between us.

Finally, in the writing of this book, I had the privilege of working with Laura Yorke, who edited the manuscript. In the process, I not only benefited from her extraordinary talent as an editor but was also able to come full circle with a key part of my story. One of the most important milestones on my journey was reading *Younger Next Year* and being exposed to its powerful message that through regular exercise, we can dramatically alter the shape of our aging/fitness curve. Laura, as it turned out, edited *Younger Next Year* and later married one of its co-authors—and was delighted to learn how much that book had changed my life.

Prologue

I had been running for nearly 11 hours. I was still in control mentally. As I ran, I was taking stock of my body, the ground I still needed to cover, and the amount of time left until the gun went off and the finish line in the massive soccer stadium would be blocked off, physically preventing anyone from crossing after the 12-hour mark. My right hamstring had been redlining for most of the last five hours. I would run hard for a minute or so before the muscle started to spasm, calming down as I shifted to a fast walk for a count of 20. Once I started running again, the spasms would return. Periodically, like a race car driver making a pit stop, I had pulled over for lightning hamstring massages given by student physical therapists on the side of the road. It was intense, but manageable.

Half an hour earlier I had thought I was in good shape to make it. It would be close, but I would pass the sixth checkpoint, the last before the stadium, with a few minutes to spare and would then have a tight but makeable push to the finish. Then, I had come upon a hill that seemed to go on and on. I had read about these hills with no names. It was, after all, the Valley of a Thousand Hills. This one had really slowed me. I just couldn't run any part of it, watching the minutes slip by on my Garmin and with them my margin of error.

The checkpoint was now less than a quarter of a mile away. I desperately tried to make back some of the lost time. It was, I thought, a lost cause. Then, I heard someone shout from the side of the road to pick up the pace, that there were still two minutes left to make it. I began to speed up, hoping that maybe there was enough time for a miracle.

I was 56 years old as I ran that day, taking on the world's largest and oldest ultramarathon despite being late to endurance sports and in so many ways unsuited for this challenge. This is the story of how I found myself there and of the adventures that were yet to come.

CHAPTER 1

Free T-Shirt

I ran my first race for the free t-shirt. I was 17, and a friend's father owned a restaurant that was sponsoring a local 10K. The friend invited two of my brothers and me to enter. We wouldn't have to pay a fee, and we would get a free t-shirt in the bargain. It seemed like too good a deal to pass up.

My brothers and I were tennis players. They were younger and better than me, both destined to play Division 1 college tennis and to complete a year on the pro tour, while my tennis career would top out at a Division 3 school.

We didn't fear the physical challenge of the race. Indeed, I don't recall giving it a moment's thought beforehand. I got the t-shirt and wore it for years after that. The race itself provided far less satisfaction. After four miles of running, I was wiped out and ended up walking the final two miles. My legs ached for the next week. More lasting was the frustration I felt over not having been able to run the whole distance, a feeling that would linger below the surface for the next 30 years. In the end, that would be the most useful thing I got out of my quest for the free t-shirt.

My brother Farley crushed the race, finishing it in less than 47 minutes, a highly respectable time, especially for a first timer who didn't even train. His success made me believe that a runner was something you either were or were not. I was, I concluded, not a runner.

I left running alone for a few years after that. Then, with college over and my tennis career behind me, I started to think about my fitness options. Over time I had realized that I never really enjoyed the game of tennis, but playing with my brothers and my tennis friends had given me a sense of identity. I was proud that I could play a sport decently well, and I liked the athletic life-style—training every day. With tennis gone, I was losing the identity and the structure that it had provided. I also noticed that my weight was slowly creeping up, and I became determined to do something about it.

In that first year after college, I decided to give running a shot. I was living in Jerusalem at the time, where I was a first-year law student. All my courses were in Hebrew, a language that I had only begun studying in college. I was able to manage the lectures and the reading, becoming progressively more confident as the year went on, but I never got over my fear of being called on and having to answer in front of my classmates, with my heavy accent and frequent grammar mistakes. I thought running might help relieve some of the stress.

I created a loop route that was remarkably scenic—past the national concert hall, a luxury hotel, the Israel Museum, the Knesset (Israel's parliament building), and then through a park before a short stretch past a small cemetery to my apartment building. I always ran it at night, when the relative quiet and the lights from Jerusalem's various hilltop neighborhoods gave the scene a kind of magical quality. Someone told me I should breathe through my nose when I ran, and I followed that advice. It was, I was told, a way to avoid throat discomfort when running in colder temperatures. It was a challenge—I always felt slightly out of breath—but unthinkingly I did it. It felt good to sweat again, and, all-in-all, I enjoyed it. I survived the year, passing all my courses, but after I moved back to the states to finish law school, the route and the magic—and the intense school anxiety for that matter—were gone. I stopped running entirely.

I did find my replacement sport, however. Weightlifting became my passion and provided me with a new sense of athletic identity. I liked the changes that I saw in my body, the thrill of getting stronger and achieving new max lifts. Lifting weights and seeing your body develop over time was like being a young teenager again.

Over time I started to get pulled more to powerlifting, which had more structure than simply lifting to build muscle. Powerlifting is based on achieving max lifts for the bench press, squat, and deadlift. I applied myself diligently to all three. I was already taking bench press seriously and now focused on the other two as well. With powerlifting, my sense of growth came not just from increasing muscle mass, something which at the end of the day was hard to quantify, but also from seeing my lifting totals go up from month to month.

I made steady progress, much of it coming during law school, where lifting provided a welcome diversion from my studies. My deadlift got increasingly stronger, and during my third year I broke 400 pounds. Though I hated doing it, the squat was also a strong lift for me. I focused on getting to a weight that I could lift for five controlled repetitions rather than a one-rep-max, fearful that going for broke on a single lift could end badly. I got to 365 pounds for five reps, but the bench press was where I put most of my focus. I wanted to bench 200 pounds and, after achieving that, 225 pounds. Two hundred twenty-five is the weight used for the bench press event in the NFL combine each year, with the number of repetitions providing a basic measure of athletic strength. I got that 225 bench and steadily increased the number of reps, until that glorious day in 1987 when I did it 13 times. But the big goal, to the point of obsession, became a 300-pound bench.

Running reared its head briefly in 1992, when I was persuaded by my girlfriend Leisha to enter a local 10K with her. She was an outstanding runner, having once broken 37 minutes over that distance, and would no doubt be competitive in the race. Perhaps, I thought, this would be my chance to redeem my failure from more than a decade earlier and I agreed to sign up. As I had when I was 17, I awaited the day of the race without doing any training at all. We had decided to walk to the start, which was near where we were living, but misjudged the distance. A few minutes into the walk it became clear that we were not going to get there in time. Leisha started running, but I decided that I would skip the race and just get there to watch her finish. She ran more than a mile, made it for the start, and finished in under 40 minutes, taking second place among the women. It was a remarkable performance. For me, the 10K redemption was not to be.

I continued to chase the 300-pound bench, though. Twice I got up to 290, but I always seemed to run into an injury, a cold, or a busy period at work that interfered with my workouts at a critical juncture. And then, inevitably, I came to realize that the 300 bench was not going to happen. I got married in 1993 when I was 30—to that dazzling 10K runner. Our four kids (Danny, Abby, Tali, and Aaron) were born in 1994, 1995, 1997 and 1999, so powerlifting had to take a back seat. I was still committed to maintaining muscle mass but could no longer afford four 45-minute lifting sessions per week at the gym. It was a struggle. There were occasional breaks in training, sometimes for months. I gave up on squatting and the deadlift entirely. They seemed too punishing on my body, and the squat required too much equipment for a home gym, a convenient excuse to give it up since I had never really enjoyed it, anyway. I made peace with the occasional lunchtime or weekend workout. Life was moving on.

CHAPTER 2

Fast Forward

My father passed away when I was nearly 46, and later that year, I flew out to Las Vegas to help my mother downsize. There was furniture that needed to be moved to storage or to Goodwill and a garage to empty. I was joined by my 25-year-old brother Josh (the youngest member of my 7-sibling family) and my 19-year old nephew Jason. The two of them were outstanding athletes. Josh had played high school baseball, soccer and basketball, and Jason was playing college soccer.

As we moved pieces of furniture through the house, onto the truck, and from there to its final destination, I discovered that I could keep up. I still had much of my strength from powerlifting, and I still had drive. In the afternoon, the two of them stopped to take a nap while I kept going. I realized, though, that I was coasting off my past training and the effects would not last forever. If I wanted to remain physically active, and I now understood that I did, I would need to get more serious about things.

A few months later, I met Jason Schwartz. Jason was a big guy, a former football lineman in high school, and I had seen him around the neighborhood. He was about 6'2", and I had noticed how he had gone from thick to lean. I asked how he had done it. He told me that his wife was a runner and that she had always encouraged him to try the sport. He had resisted. He believed he was too big and had explained to her that everything hurt when he tried to run. But weighing almost 300 pounds and not feeling that well, he decided to give running a try, hoping that it would help him get his weight down. He had started with two minutes of running followed by two minutes of walking and had built up from there. By the time I met him, he had lost 100 pounds and had run a marathon.

It all sounded remarkable to me. Jason's excuses had been mine as well. Running, I had believed, was not for guys my size. I decided to give running a fresh try. I started with the two minute/two minute strategy from Jason and slowly built up until I was able to run for 30 minutes straight. A few months later I saw a notice about a local running class given by two women, Lisa Reichman and Julie Sapper. The class consisted of a Sunday long run with the group, a lecture every Monday night, and a shorter run during the week. The goal was to run the Veterans Day 10K in Washington, D. C. that November, in about two months' time. At that first session, Lisa and Julie talked about running at a conversational pace, one that was easy enough to allow you to manage a conversation while you ran. Though it now seems so obvious, I was amazed to discover that by slowing down I could run longer and with less discomfort. I was still doing the nose breathing thing from more than 25 years earlier, still hated it, and I asked them about it. They dismissed the practice immediately. They told me to breathe normally through my mouth and not to worry about the temperature of the air, which was a relief.

For one of the Monday sessions, an orthopedic surgeon came in to lecture on avoiding running injuries. The real theme of his presentation, however, was maintaining health and fitness over the long term. Early in his PowerPoint he put up two graphs. The first showed aging as most of us think about it: hitting our physical/athletic peak in our 20s and then beginning a steady decline into our 70s or 80s. The second presented aging as we *can* experience it: maintaining performance close to our peak for decades, potentially into our 80s. There would be decline, to be sure, but at a far more gradual rate than in the classic graph. To illustrate his point, he put up slides showing a 91-year-old completing a marathon and a 74-year-old running the distance in less than three hours. I found the whole thing mind-blowing—and inspiring.

I did the long runs with the group every Sunday but had trouble fitting in the mid-week runs. Still, even just doing a single run per week, I was able to steadily increase my distance and a couple of weeks before the race, finished our longest scheduled training run of five miles. The Veterans Day 10K was a major local running event with over 2,300 participants. When the gun went off for the start, everyone around me surged forward and I could feel the energy. I ran the entire distance, finishing at 1:07:50. I got increasingly excited over the last fraction of a mile as I could see the finish come into view, erasing my failure from nearly 30 years before. Lisa had been all over the course looking for her students and running with each of us for a short while. When the group gathered after the finish, Julie handed me a banana with strict instructions to eat it, something about restoring my potassium. Her seriousness and concern amused me. We all stood in a circle, exchanging stories and basking in our successes.

CHAPTER 3

What Next

In the weeks and months following the race, I continued to run. I stayed focused on the 10K distance, but now that I had actually run a whole race, I decided to work on improving my time. I wanted to break one hour for the distance—my new 300-pound bench. I entered a race in April and then another in May. I came up short in both. While I didn't give up on the idea of breaking one hour, I was also starting to realize that I was never going to be fast. At 6', 220 pounds, I did not exactly have a classic runner's build. I started to think about the possibility of running longer distances.

I found a 7-mile race—an odd distance I've never seen again—and entered it. It was a hot day and my first exposure to run-walk—running for a predetermined amount of time, walking for a set period, and repeating. As the race progressed, I noticed a couple of racers who would barrel by me at a fast pace and whom I would then jog past as they walked. Then the cycle would repeat itself. I found the whole thing silly. It seemed like far less strain to just maintain a constant running speed. One of these runners, who I mentally nicknamed Raging Bull, was a burly guy who was breathing harder than I had ever heard at a race. As I rounded one corner, I came upon him lying on the ground and being attended to by EMT's. If I had any doubt about the wisdom of run-walk by that point in the race, the image of Raging Bull on the ground, completely spent, erased it.

I started to wonder about even longer distances and specifically about the half marathon. We were living in Maryland, and the area had a well-known race called the Parks Half Marathon. The course was point-to-point, starting in Rockville and finishing in Bethesda. It was net downhill, and, as the name implied, was mostly through the local park system. Race day was set for September 11, 2011, the tenth anniversary of 9/11. As I studied the race website, I noticed that there was a course time limit of 2:45, which translated into a 12:36 per mile pace. That pace would, I believed, be a stretch for me.

I found a training plan online and started to extend my long runs. The plan called for a longest run of ten miles, and I began to build toward that. Along the way, I developed pain in my right calf. I researched it online; it seemed like a strain rather than a tear. I took a week off running and also bought some kinesiology tape, which seemed to help, and then resumed training. At night, before going to bed, I would take out my iPad and study the race map. Imagining covering all that ground excited me; yet, at the same time I continued to worry about being able to maintain the 12:36 pace. The map review became my go-to distraction from the stresses of the day.

From the race website, I learned that there would be pace groups, each led by a runner whose goal would be to maintain the pace needed to achieve a particular finishing time. I thought that could be an interesting way to take the constant stress of maintaining a proper pace out of the equation. The question became which group to choose. I wanted something of a cushion between me and a 2:45 finishing time, which left me with a choice between the 2:20 and 2:30 groups. I was tempted by 2:20 but worried that it might be too ambitious and cause me to blow up early. I opted for 2:30.

I checked in race morning and headed to the start area. I looked around at the other racers as I waited. Apparently, half-marathon fitness did not require the physique of the stereotypical lean marathoner, which I found reassuring as I waited for the start, all 220 pounds of me. I grew more and more nervous as the race start drew nearer. This would be nearly double the distance of my longest race. They started us in waves, and my pace group was in the third wave. When it was our turn, we began running, heading out onto the city streets that made up the first couple of miles of the course before we would turn into the park system.

After some jitters I began to settle into a rhythm. We entered the park, and I found it easy to keep up with the group. As we passed the three-mile marker, I felt myself getting pulled forward and decided that I could comfortably go a little faster. I moved ahead and set out on my own. The terrain really was mild, either nice and flat or gently downhill. I was startled to occasionally encounter pairs of runners, almost always women, running and chatting like it was just another low-key training run to be enjoyed with a friend. I really admired their calm, in contrast to my continued nervousness about whether I would be able to finish the race in the allotted time.

The miles ticked by. My body held together—no calf pain—and I was maintaining a pace that would have me finish in slightly less than 2:30. When I saw the marker for mile 10, I knew that I would make it. I kept going, tired but confident. After the mile 12 marker, I passed a group of Brownies handing out small American flags to carry across the finish line in remembrance of 9/11. Minutes later I crossed, flag in hand. I felt a surge of excitement. It had been a stretch goal for me, and I had accomplished it.

I had stayed ahead of my pace group, finishing just a shade above 2:25. After all my anxiety about the cut-off, I was delighted to realize that I had been able to hold an 11:06 pace. I had experienced something I had heard described as "race day magic"—that things that seemed impossible during training, whether speed or distance or both, could be within reach when you added in the variable of the excitement of a race.

CHAPTER 4

Triathlon

A few months after that first 10K with Lisa and Julie's running class, I came across my handout of the slides from the orthopedic surgeon's presentation. I found the two fitness graphs that had so struck me—the one showing steady physical decline beginning in the late 20s and the other with almost stable fitness into the 80s—and realized that they came from a book called *Younger Next Year*. I bought a copy and eagerly read it. The graphs were accompanied by these stirring words:

> You do not have to get old the way you think. You can do all the same things, almost the same way. Bike, ski, make love. Make sense! Roughly the same energy, roughly the same pleasure. Roughly the same guy. In fact, if you're a bit of a mess right now, you can become a radically *better* guy over the next five years and *then* level off. (Crowley & Lodge, 2007, p. 6)

Although there were other aspects to it, the key practical takeaway from *Younger Next Year* was that achieving the desired aging curve required a person to exercise six days a week, at least 45 minutes per session. I resolved to do exactly that, fitting the weekday workouts into my morning after the kids left for school or during my lunch hour, taking Saturdays off, and doing a Sunday morning workout. But I knew that running six days a week was not going to cut it. I didn't enjoy running enough to do it that often, and, in any event, it was simply going to be too much wear and tear for my body. I needed to look at cross-training.

I started by adding in stationary bike sessions, with the occasional spinning class mixed in from time to time. I then decided to try swimming at a local county pool. I showed up with a baggy, knee-length beach bathing suit, and when I started swimming, it blew up like a balloon. I didn't even try freestyle. For 45 minutes, I swam a snail-slow breaststroke back and forth, happy just to be able to complete an entire workout.

Based on the results of that first trip to the county pool, I was confident I could fill out my six-day-a-week exercise routine with a mix of running, biking, and swimming. Although my 45-minute breaststroke session was enough to persuade me to add swimming to my schedule, I hoped to do better than what I had managed that first day. I knew freestyle was faster, so I started out weaving in a single lap of freestyle, after a long breaststroke warmup, and then alternated one lap of free style with four laps of breaststroke. I kept increasing the ratio and, after a few months, was able to do longer stretches of straight freestyle. And, of course, I did something about that bathing suit.

I have always been a reader and over the years have tended to get very interested in a single subject and then to focus my reading for an extended period on books within that area. I now turned my reading almost entirely over to fitness. I started to learn about triathlons – races of varying distances with swim, bike and run legs. They ranged from Sprint (typically a swim of between 300 and 500 yards, a bike of 10-12 miles, and a 5K run), Olympic (a 1.5K swim, a 40K bike, and a 10K run), Half-Ironman or 70.3 (a 1.2-mile swim, 56-mile bike, and a half marathon) to Ironman or 140.6 (a 2.4-mile swim, 112-mile bike and a full marathon). Since I was already cross-training using the three triathlon sports, it seemed exciting to take on an actual race. The Sprint distance seemed doable and yet, at the same time, far more daunting than a straightforward 10K.

There was also something about that name *triathlon* and the mystique it carried that drew me in. I thought it sounded cool—achieving proficiency in three different disciplines and stringing them together in a single race. Of course, the mystique really came from the longest and most famous of the conventional triathlon distances: the Ironman. It seemed to be the ultimate measure of human fitness, a race that pushed people to the breaking point. For those of us who came of age during the era of Wide World of Sports, the popular sports variety show in the years before ESPN, one of the most gripping episodes had featured Julie Moss's dramatic finish at the Ironman 1982 World Championship. Moss had staggered toward the finish line, her body severely dehydrated and seizing up. Persevering, she had crawled the last few feet to finish.

Triathlons opened the door to a whole new world of study. I learned that the race itself consisted not just of the three events but also of the transitions between them. There was also a need to focus on taking in enough calories and liquids during the race. As the Julie Moss experience showed, there could be serious consequences on race day for failing to nail proper nutrition. And then, perhaps most fun of all, there was the fascinating world of triathlon gear. A budding triathlete would want to think about what to wear, taking into account that you would be in the water, on a bike, and running during a single race. At a minimum you would want a pair of tri shorts, which were like bike shorts but with a smaller pad that promised to be both comfortable and quick drying. A separate tri-top would provide added warmth during the swim and was close-fitting enough (and equipped with pockets in the back) to double as a bike shirt, yet comfortable enough to stay on for the run. The one-piece tri-suit, in theory, gave you both things in a single item of clothing though, as I later learned, required a fair amount of gymnastics to pee out of in a porta-potty. For colder water, a triathlon wetsuit would also be needed though deciding which type (long sleeves, short sleeves, no sleeves) generated its own list of pros and cons.

I found a race for the summer and signed up. It consisted of a 300-yard pool swim, an 11-mile bike, and then a 5K. It seemed like a perfect first race; both the swim and the bike were on the short side of what I had seen for sprint distance races. Also, I had started to learn about open water swims, which sounded daunting. The term *washing machine* kept coming up to describe the churning effect of swimmers colliding as the race began, and there were some horror stories about athletes drowning. I didn't want to have the stress of open water be part of my first triathlon experience.

The combination of running and biking in a single race added another dimension. Nobody seemed particularly concerned about the physical challenge of going from the swim to the bike, since swimming was primarily upper body and biking primarily lower body. Going from the bike to the run was different. Although the specific leg muscles did not fully overlap, a bike ride left your legs pumped up, which could feel awkward at the start of a run. To get used to this, triathletes were advised to incorporate "bricks" into their workouts—a bike ride followed by a quick transition to a run. (The name *brick* came from the way that your legs felt after you got off the bike and began your run.) I talked Leisha into joining me for the race. She remained a strong runner, biked occasionally, and had much better swimming form than I did. I explained bricks to her, and we ended up doing a single one before the race. One week before race day, we rode for a few miles, put the bikes away, and then ran for a couple of miles. The transition from the bike to the run had been effortless, and I couldn't figure out what all the fuss was about.

We awoke race morning to what promised to be a very hot day, with the high reaching into the low 90's. The pool swim turned out to be a logistical nightmare. The organizers put swimmers into their own lanes, having them enter in bib order, beginning after the ten or so elite racers had finished their swim leg. We had entered late and had high bib numbers, so it was well over an hour before we got into the pool. Still, it was fascinating to watch the different swim styles. Nearly everyone swam freestyle. Some did so beautifully, with nicely executed flip turns. But there was also breaststroke, back stroke, side stroke, and even one dog paddle. If I had been intimidated before the race by my image of the athletic proficiency of the racers, that feeling was gone by the time I got into the pool.

When it was finally my turn, I climbed in and started. I felt great and had no problem beginning with freestyle. That was the high point of my athletic accomplishment for the race. Of the 18 competitors in my age group, I finished 7th for the swim. For the bike leg, I was using a mountain bike I really liked. I knew it wasn't an ideal choice, but it was comfortable and I didn't see any reason to stress over it. My tennis coach growing up was a hard-nosed traditionalist, and he was derisive about the temptation to fixate on equipment. He used to say that if you were good, you could play with a frying pan.

I plodded along on the bike. The loop course was mostly flat, but it still took me slightly over 50 minutes to complete the 11 miles, which worked out to a 13. 4 mph pace. I pulled up to transition and dismounted, happy to have finished the bike leg. I racked the bike and changed my shoes, then stood up and started moving toward the exit to begin the run. I could tell immediately that something was different. *This* was the brick feeling I had read about. I immediately realized that what I had constructed as a brick workout was nothing more than a short bike warmup leading to a short run.

The brick feeling lingered for quite a while. Even when it passed, I was spent. The temperature was in the 90s, and I plodded along, completing the leg in 36:10. To my great pleasure, I had finished my first triathlon.

Leisha, who had been far more competitive within her age group than I, was bitten by the bug, and we found another race for later that summer. This one had a similar pool swim, a far hillier bike ride, and then a relatively flat 3-mile run. My bike leg was even slower—something that I was able to blame on the course profile—but my run pace improved dramatically to 10:10 per mile. With the racing season over, I was happy to have solidified my self-identification as a triathlete and looked forward to continuing the next summer.

CHAPTER 5

Speed, Sort Of

Although I really hadn't found any pleasure in either race, other than the accomplishment of finishing, I was committed to the triathlon. I felt that it gave structure to my whole workout routine. There was a purposefulness to it which really resonated with me. The triathlon gave me a feeling that I was working out *for* something, that I was on a journey toward a destination. Otherwise, I worried that I would just be tempted to mark off my 45-minute sessions, and that ultimately, without the pull of ever-increasing goals, my whole approach to fitness might become unsatisfying — and I could find myself right back where I was, before the running class.

Identifying a goal and going after it was an approach that I had cultivated in the non-fitness aspects of my life as well. I had challenged myself multiple times since completing that year of law school in Hebrew. That challenge had included getting a master's in international law at night, when I first considered changing the direction of my legal career away from commercial litigation. Later, I did make a change, completing 32 semester hours of biology and chemistry over a 3-year period to qualify to take the patent bar exam and become a patent attorney. I had also been able to overlap my science studies with the research and writing of my first book, achieving a long-cherished goal of becoming an author.

While I looked ahead to more triathlons the next summer, I wasn't yet done with the 10K distance and the desire to break one-hour. There were still a few running events on the calendar before winter set in. One of these was the Home Run 10K, located a little more than a mile from my house. It passed over what running writers describe as "rolling hills"— fairly long and gentle inclines and declines, though they didn't seem so gentle at that point in my running journey. The race was scheduled for October, and I decided to give it a shot.

As the Home Run approached, I thought about my race strategy. I had learned about splits (negative, even, and positive), which required you to divide a particular distance in half and then focus on your time for each half of the race. The negative split, which everyone seemed to agree was ideal, required you to run the second half of a race slightly faster than the first, That, for a beginning runner like me, seemed counter-intuitive, since I had assumed you would inevitably get progressively slower the longer you ran. An even split was, as the name implied, one in which the two halves were run at the same pace. And the positive split consisted of a faster first half and a slightly slower second half. In my continuing quest to break one hour in the

10K, I had become convinced that I would have to run a negative split.

But having tried and failed several times with negative splits to achieve a sub-one-hour 10K, I was re-thinking my strategy. I wondered whether a focus on negative splits was leading me to hold back too much in the first half of the race, expecting to make it up with a much speedier second half. I mentioned my pacing challenge to Leisha. In putting up her impressive 10K times, she had always run instinctively and had never worried about any of this. She offered me a simpler approach: "Just go balls out until you can't anymore."

"What the hell," I thought, it's worth a try.

On race morning, I woke up with a slight cold. I arrived at the Home Run feeling deflated and tempted to just skip the whole thing. Nevertheless, I moved into the start area and waited for the race to begin. When we got the signal, I began running, still arguing with myself over whether to continue. It would be so easy to run to the side and step out of the race, but I just couldn't do it and continued with the pack. I knew I would have to average a 9:43 pace to break one hour, and I focused on trying to keep a bit ahead of that as I moved down a long stretch of rolling hills, slightly out of breath from the speed but the effects of my cold forgotten. As I crossed a timing mat at the turnaround that marked the half-way point of the race, I could see that I was ahead of my goal pace. This time I really had a shot. I found myself running stride for stride with a woman who was holding the same pace. That was a huge help. I now focused on keeping up with her rather than simply trying to do what my watch was telling me to do. In the last mile I felt able to pull ahead and crossed at 57:20, thrilled not only to have broken one hour but to have crushed it—and on a day when I had not felt my best. It was my crucial first experience with successfully ignoring that inner voice that runners invariably struggle with, telling them to stop or slow down.

I still had one more 10K to run for the season, a Turkey Trot in nearby Bethesda that I ran with Leisha. The course there promised to be even hillier, but having now broken one hour, I felt this was a standard I needed to maintain. I turned in an even better performance, finishing in 55:19. With a year of endurance sports under my belt, I was able to look back with satisfaction at having run multiple 10Ks, at having broken the one-hour mark twice, at having run a half marathon, and at having finished two Sprint triathlons. Amazed that I had been able to do things that would have been unthinkable just a couple of years earlier, I wondered what else I might be able to achieve. I pondered that next goal for a few months and then decided. I would try for a full marathon.

CHAPTER 6

Marine Corps

The obvious first marathon for a DC-area runner is the Marine Corp Marathon (MCM). It has been around since the 1970s and is the fourth largest marathon in the U. S. and the ninth largest in the world. It has a great course: starting at the Pentagon in Virginia, winding its way through D. C., and finishing at the Iwo Jima memorial. The problem I soon realized was that signing up for a big city marathon like MCM was not like registering for a local 10K. MCM registration had filled up the day it opened months earlier, and signing up now was not an option.

I looked around at other races and remembered the Potomac River Run (PRR), which Jason Schwartz and another friend had finished. PRR was a local, low-key race. It typically had just a couple of hundred runners, who would run out and back twice along a slightly more than 6-mile stretch of canal bank near the Potomac River. Although I would have preferred MCM, I had decided to run a marathon for the fall of 2012 and did not want to defer that dream another year. I signed up for PRR, downloaded a 20-week training plan, and got to work. I would be on my own for this challenge. Leisha continued to excel at the 10K and had no desire to take on longer distances.

After I had signed up for Parks, everything about the race had energized my training in the months leading up to race day. There was the drama of the new distance, the anxiety about being able to maintain the minimum pace, and the course map that I could review every night while I imagined myself doing something that I had always thought impossible. PRR just wasn't doing any of that for me. Weeks into my training, I stumbled across the MCM bib transfer policy, one that is unique among big city marathons. In recognition of the fact that so many MCM runners are in the military and that many are subject to being deployed sometime after sign-up and before race day, the organizers open a window a few months before the race for registered runners to sell their entry (race bib) to another runner. I couldn't believe my good fortune. I went online the day the transfer window opened, found someone looking to sell their bib, and just like that I was in.

In an instant, I was energized about running my first marathon. One major problem remained, though. MCM was scheduled for three weeks earlier than PRR. That meant that I was going to have to figure out a way to cut three weeks out of my plan and still be ready on race day. I knew I couldn't eliminate the taper, the final two weeks of training when the run distances are dramatically cut, with the goal of delivering you to the starting line fresh and fully recovered from any lingering injuries. I had read time and again how important a good taper was for race performance. I also wanted to keep my longest run, set for 20 miles, which seemed common to virtually every marathon training program. I also knew that I couldn't get to that number too quickly; my body needed to gradually adjust to the increasing load if I were to avoid injury. So, I trimmed a little here and a little there and, with that, I was off.

Like Parks, MCM also had a minimum pace required for runners to stay in the race, a generous 14-minutes per mile. Runners who were not maintaining the minimum pace by mile 17 or 20 would be diverted onto the sidewalks and not certified as official finishers. Given my experience at Parks, where in the end the minimum pace had not proven to be a challenge, I was not concerned about beating the cut-offs. Instead, I worried about the distance itself. Like most new runners, the idea of doubling my longest distance—in this case going from a half marathon to a full—was daunting. I knew how I had felt at the finish line at Parks, and the idea of essentially turning around at the finish and running all the way back to the start, which the race announcer had joked that runners were free to do, seemed impossible. I understood that pacing and training were key. I had been physically spent at the end of Parks both because that was the distance I trained for and because I had maintained a pace that allowed me to optimize my speed over that distance. This time I would be building up the length of my long runs *and* would moderate my pace so as not to blow up before the finish. It made sense in theory, but visualizing it with all that training still in the future was a different matter.

Over the next few weeks, I methodically executed my revised training plan. I steadily built up my distance and, with less than six weeks to go before the race, I headed out for a 15-mile run. The run went fine, but when I made the final turn toward my neighborhood, I felt a twinge in my right knee. Instantly I felt hobbled, unable to run without pain, and walked the remaining few hundred yards home. I assumed it was no big deal—just one of the myriad aches and pains that come and go during a run, with no lasting effect. But over the next few days it became clear that this actually was a problem. I would rest for a few days and then try to get back out and run. Each time, the pain would return within a few miles, and I would have to end the workout. The weeks were passing and with them my scheduled long runs of 16, 18 and 20 miles. MCM was clearly not going to happen.

I had begun a new job at a start-up company as its general counsel a few weeks earlier and learned that one of my new co-workers had previously completed several Ironman triathlons. I explained my situation to him. He told me the same thing had happened to him before his first marathon. He had dealt with it by going to a physical therapist who had recommended a change in shoe style. He had taken the advice, resumed his training, and completed his race. That was tantalizing. I asked for the number of the physical therapist, made contact, and the next day had my appointment. The PT got me up on a treadmill and watched me run. Right away he made several suggestions. He wanted me to shorten my arm swing, i.e. to keep my hands near my waist and to restrict their travel to just a few inches forward of my body and a few inches back. He also told me that I needed to increase my turnover, i.e. the frequency of my foot strikes. He explained that this would generate less force on the knee joint. And then we came to the shoes. He looked at them closely. He felt that the arch was wrong for me and told me to switch to a different model from the same brand, with a milder arch. I was ecstatic. I planned to work on the arm swing and turnover rate but knew it would be hard to maintain those changes during the inevitable fatigue of long runs or a race. Shoes were a different matter entirely. All you had to do was buy them, lace them up, and you were good to go.

A mere 11 days remained until Marine Corps. All the long runs on my schedule above 15 miles had come and gone, and I was now supposed to be in the taper, where my longest remaining run was six miles. The physical therapist was a serious marathoner, and I asked him what he thought about the race. I described my pre-injury training, and he told me that he thought I could do it. He advised me to simply resume my plan at its current point rather than trying to go back and make up any of the missed long runs. Two days later I had the new shoes and resumed running, attentive to the arm swing and turnover suggestions. I was pain-free but unsure whether I had solved anything or if it was just because the runs were so short.

I thought more about the race and how to approach it. A while earlier I had read *Galloway's Book on Running* by former Olympian Jeff Galloway, and in it he had preached the run-walk method for which he has become famous. He claimed, among other things, that a proper run-walk strategy—e.g., running one mile and then walking for one minute—could double the maximum distance a runner could complete.

I had been dismissive of run-walk, both based on what I had seen at the Baltimore 7-miler and out of a feeling that it was somehow a less authentic way to race. Still, I knew that MCM was going to be a major challenge given my interrupted training, and I couldn't entirely dismiss Galloway. I decided to compromise. In studying the race map, I noticed that the water stations were about 2.5 miles apart. In all my prior races, including Parks, I had run every step, including through the water stations. I would take a cup from a volunteer without breaking stride, pinch the mouth of the cup to minimize spilling, and then try to consume as much as possible while moving out of the station and back into the flow of runners. Inevitably, it had been messy, though it had made me feel good about my effort. This time, I decided, I would walk through the aid stations. That would give me the benefit of a short walking break while preserving my sense of the authenticity of a fully run race since walking while drinking was hardly unusual.

The night before the race, I laid out all my stuff. Logistics was, for me, another great joy of racing. I loved the pre-race planning: trying to make the best possible decisions about the gear I would need and making sure it was all in the right place so that I would not forget anything as I headed out in the early morning darkness. Much of my planning was based on things I had read rather than on my own race experiences since this would be my first—and I assumed only—marathon. I knew it would be chilly at the start and had read about wearing a layer of warm clothes over your race attire that you could throw away. For that, I had chosen an old pair of sweatpants and a hoodie.

When I was taking the running class, Lisa and Julie had discouraged the idea of running with headphones. Part of it reflected a purist approach to running, one in which the joy of being in motion in nature was all the entertainment you needed. They were also concerned about the safety of running outside and not being fully aware of your surroundings, particularly for female runners out in the early morning or at night. Most races at that time had a no-headphones policy, the theory being that a runner with headphones would be unable to hear if another runner was trying to pass. After initially following Lisa and Julie's advice, I had gotten used to headphones and couldn't imagine training without music or an audiobook. I had a long day ahead of me—assuming all went well with my knee—and really wanted to be able to listen to something other than the voice in my head. I was relieved when I saw on the MCM website that, while headphones were discouraged, they were not prohibited.

On race morning, I got on the subway not far from my house. I saw other racers and, at each stop, more joined. I could feel the excitement building. By the time we reached the Pentagon, the cars were packed. Hundreds of us exited the train and joined with other runners, all streaming toward the start area. After a brief security check, I found myself in the wide expanse of the Pentagon's parking lot, among a sea of runners either milling around or sitting in groups. There was an unmistakable air of excited, nervous anticipation. As the start of the race grew closer, I knew I needed to squeeze in a pee. The porta-potty lines were daunting, and it seemed like finding a discrete alternative at the Pentagon of all places was not going to be possible. Then I caught sight of a group of male runners who had found concealment behind a giant, spooled-up firehose, and I rushed over and joined them. We all shared mischievous smiles, having squeezed in our pre-race pee without the nightmare of the long lines.

I then moved to where runners were lining up in a long parade that ultimately led to the start. With 20 minutes or so until the race cannon would go off, I stood there, hood still in place, absorbing the high-energy music blasting throughout the area. The hoodie, I decided, was perfect for this moment, creating a cocoon of serenity amid thousands of runners while allowing me to take in the excitement all around. Right before the start, a pair of Marine Osprey aircraft did a flyover. Then came the national anthem and a blast from a howitzer to mark the official start. Slowly, the crowd snaked forward. I shucked my sweatpants and hoodie as we moved, throwing them off to the side. With more than 20,000 runners, it took minutes to get to the start. And then, in an instant, we were off.

The need to pee before the start of a long race really was a thing, perhaps psychological as much as anything else. I had been lucky to find the spooled fire hose, but others clearly had not been as fortunate. Not long after leaving the Pentagon, we briefly entered a tree-lined parkway, and dozens of runners headed off the course toward the trees for a quick pee, to a general chorus of good-natured laughter from the rest of us.

We moved through the streets of Rosslyn, Virginia: large office buildings on either side, enthusiastic spectators on the sidewalks, and thousands of runners crammed in between. As at Parks, I was relieved to see that not everyone in a marathon had that thin, slight, classic runner's build. Indeed, there was no shortage of folks who looked quite unsuited for the task ahead of us. Yet here they were chugging along, no doubt on target to turn in a much faster performance than I, assuming I could even cover the distance on my suspect knee and insufficient training base.

I reached the first water station and walked it as planned. Shortly after mile 4, we crossed Key Bridge into D. C., a first scenic moment. We headed through a several-mile loop around a reservoir and then along the Potomac River toward the Capital Mall, which we would reach later in the race. The miles ticked by, and the knee continued to hold. When I passed 10 miles, I felt that I had accomplished something, and I pulled out my phone to text the milestone to Leisha.

The crowds had been thick on both sides of the course nearly from the beginning, and the cacophony they created was a powerful motivator. The signs as well were a welcome distraction: "worst parade ever," "this seemed like a good idea when you signed up months ago," and "this is a lot of work for a free banana." I had been warned by a friend that Haines Point, a jutting area of parks and a golf course which we would reach at mile 11 and not leave until mile 15, was the one quiet part of the entire route. As I left Haines Point,

I sent another short update text to Leisha, letting her know that I had just finished 15 miles. I was now at the distance of my longest training run. Every mile from here on out would be a new personal best but also unchartered territory with uncertain consequences for my body. The next five miles were the most scenic of the race, which came as a welcome distraction as I crossed into virgin terrain. First, we ran along the Potomac River tidal basin and the Jefferson Memorial. We then came near to the Lincoln Memorial before turning toward the US Capital Building two miles away, passing the Washington Monument and the Smithsonian Museum buildings located along Capital Mall.

With the tour of historic DC behind me, I experienced some deflation. I passed the 20-mile marker before reaching the bridge, which meant that I still had 10K worth of distance to go. I had read a lot about marathoners "hitting the wall," which meant reaching a point in the race when your energy stores are depleted and you become overwhelmed by feelings of fatigue and negativity. Runners who hit the wall might be forced to walk, to slow down so much that they might as well be walking, or in extreme cases to drop out of the race. Some argued that it was an experience that nearly all marathoners had, while others claimed that proper training could eliminate the wall. Since I knew I hadn't properly trained, the image of the wall loomed large for me. While the precise point where runners could be expected to encounter it varied, the 20-mile mark was frequently identified as the spot. I passed 20 miles and continued to feel fine, tight hamstrings but otherwise no overwhelming sense of exhaustion or depression.

After the bridge, we did a 2-mile loop through Crystal City. The densely packed crowds seemed especially loud, if not frenzied. Perhaps that was because I was among the back-of-the-packers, and we all looked to be especially in need of encouragement as we covered those last painful miles. Exiting Crystal City, we moved past the Pentagon, along the same route that I had followed that morning.

As we approached the finish, the course made a sharp turn, and we had to climb a short hill to the Iwo Jima Memorial, part of the mystique of the MCM. With the race in the bag and the finish line within sight, I decided that it would be great to accelerate up the hill and complete the race in style. But when I tried to translate that impulse into increased speed, I came up empty and could only continue to plod that last hundred yards or so. I crossed the finish line to encounter the final thing that made MCM special: a Marine lieutenant who saluted me and placed my finisher's medal over my neck. I had made it.

I wandered around the finishers' area, amused by the contrast from the morning. Before the race started, the nervous energy at the Pentagon had been palpable, but we had all walked normally, as yet unaffected by what was to come. Now it was like a scene from a zombie movie: everyone stiff-legged and awkward. Still, despite the physical discomfort, it felt extraordinary to be on the other side of the challenge, to have done something that I had once thought utterly impossible. Years before starting my running journey, I had once commented to a friend that I was as likely to walk on the moon as I was to run a marathon. I probably would have still said the same thing during the first year of my running, before Parks and the realization that my body was capable of much more than I had been asking of it. Yet, almost miraculously, here I stood, a marathon finisher's medal around my neck.

CHAPTER 7

The Magic of Two

Experts say that when running a marathon for the first time, your only goal should be to finish. After the injury and on a weak training base, certainly that was how I had approached MCM. I gave small thought to my finishing time, and even then, only to try to predict what it might be, not to set a target. I had anticipated that I might finish between 5:15 and 5:30 and in the end I did, with a time of 5:22:48. It was certainly slow, but at least I had done it.

I had approached the marathon essentially as a bucket list item, as so many runners do. I had even made that commitment to my wife, assuring her that there would be no more marathons after this one, since my weekly long runs for Marine Corps had claimed a significant part of Sunday mornings. I had meant it, and for more than a year I gave it no more thought. But as 2014 began, I started to wonder. What if I trained properly over a full 20 weeks instead of rushing things as I had when I switched to MCM from the Potomac River Run? What if I hadn't gotten hurt? What if

I had completed my long runs, including the 20-miler? If I had done all those things, could I have broken five hours?

As March approached and with it the sign-up for MCM, I decided that I had to find out. I would do the race again, this time with the right preparation, and try to finish in under five hours. As for my prior commitment to Leisha, the start-up that I had joined the prior year was based in Arizona, which required me to fly out to the company's offices every Tuesday morning and to return every Thursday night. I promised to arrange my training schedule so that I would do my long runs in the middle of the week in Arizona rather than on Sundays when I was with the family.

Part of my thinking about taking on a second marathon was my increasing dissatisfaction with my finishing time. There was, it seemed to me, something non-serious about running a marathon in more than five hours. I knew I was never going to be truly fast at any distance, but I believed I would feel a lot better about a finishing time that began with the number four. Even more, I really liked the race itself. It had been an odyssey, beginning with the quiet reflection in the darkened Pentagon parking lot, the music in the starting area as the excitement built, and then hours of racing across scenic terrain in front of spirited crowds as I fought the building fatigue to get to the finish line and earn that medal. A marathon is a journey, a long struggle toward a goal that few achieve, with emotional and physical ups and downs along the way. I wanted that experience again.

There was also something about the "one and done" or "bucket list" approach I had never liked. Lots of people seemed to have found a way to run a marathon or do some other cool thing, e.g. skydiving, once in their life. To me, it showed that they could push themselves a single time, but also that they had not really been able to change fundamentally who they were. I wanted to be a marathoner, not just someone who had once run a marathon. In place of "one and done," the number two, I felt, had a lot more magic to it: repeating the difficult thing and making it part of yourself. It was a philosophy that I have applied in other parts of my life as well, including writing (this is my third book), where my goal had been to truly become a writer rather than just a one-time author.

I decided that I would use a coach for this race, to further increase my chances for a good result. I tracked down Lisa from the running class I had taken a few years earlier and signed up with her. I could tell right away that I had made the right choice. She gave me detailed training plans that blended long runs, speed work, and hill repeats and that also addressed cross-training, stretching, and strength training. Her plan called for 16 weeks of preparation and included two 20-mile runs. I got started with a lot of enthusiasm and methodically built up my mileage base. I climbed the ladder of the prescribed long runs—first 16 miles and then 18—and everything seemed to be coming together nicely. Lisa suggested I run the Philadelphia half marathon with the goal of testing my speed. I loved the idea.

And then, as it had with the Parks half marathon and MCM, injury hit. This time it was my right calf, which started to hurt during the tenth week of the program. I persisted with the schedule, not wanting to believe that lightning had struck a second time, and completed a second 18-mile-long run. But my pace was awful, and Lisa recommended a physical therapist with great experience working with runners. When I got in to see the PT a few days later, he suspected an Achilles tendon strain and told me not to run until our next appointment the following week.

My leg saw no real improvement the next week, and Danny, the PT, told me that I might want to try dry needling. He explained that he would insert a needle into the injured area but would not be dispensing any medication. The technique was based on studies that showed that patients with my type of injury improved when injected with a variety of therapeutics, ultimately leading researchers to conclude that it was the needle and not the drug that caused the healing. I liked the idea of a dramatic intervention that could super-charge the speed of my recovery and agreed to go for it.

By the time the treatments were completed and Danny had cleared me to resume training, I had lost two full weeks. Once again, I found myself anxious as a marathon approached and scheduled long runs (this time the two 20-milers) had slipped by with no ability to do them. There were now three weeks left until race day. I still had two 16-milers on the schedule and at least I knew that if the Achilles would hold for those, I would be far better trained than the last time. For the first 16-miler, to simulate a longer run, Lisa suggested I run eight miles the day before. The 8-miler went off without a return of the calf pain, and the next day I headed out for the 16-miler. My pace was good, a refreshing change from the painfully slow runs when the calf first started to hurt and before I had gone to see Danny, but within the last half mile, I felt a tiny tinge of pain in the injured area. Worried about re-injury, I immediately shut the run down. Six days later it was time for the second 16-miler. I set out at a good pace, but at the 13-mile mark I started to feel some calf pain and again ended the run, more worried about aggravating the injury and leaving myself with no choice but to cancel the race than about short-changing my training. I was determined to get to the starting line with a shot at finishing, even if once again it meant getting there under-trained.

I discussed race strategy with Lisa. At the start of my training, based on my fastest 10K time, she believed I was capable of finishing in less than 4:30. Now, with the interruption caused by the calf injury, she thought 4:45 was a more realistic goal. She suggested that I start on the slow side and stay there for about three or four miles. I could then pick up my pace, without overdoing it, until mile 20. At that point, if I felt good, I could push the pace a little harder. I decided to add on to Lisa's plan. Some running coaches suggest having more than one goal for a race, with your most ambitious being your "A." You would then have a less ambitious "B" for the situation where things didn't go as well as expected, perhaps because of heat, cramping or just not feeling it on race day. An even slower "C" might also make sense. I liked the concept. I did not want to go in with only a single goal of breaking 4:45 and risk disappointment if I failed. A sub-4:45 was clearly my "A." I decided to make a sub-4:50 my "B" and a sub-5:00 (my original ambition) my "C." If I couldn't at least break five hours, I really would feel like the whole thing had been a failure.

I asked Lisa whether it made sense to try to do the race with a pace group. She said a pace bracelet might be a better idea. I looked into it and was fascinated. Basically, it showed your target elapsed time for every mile in the race, based on your desired finishing time. For example, for my 4:45 goal, I should be at 10:52 at the mile 1 marker, 54:21 at the mile 5 marker, 2:43:03 at the mile 15 marker, and 3:37:24 at the mile 20 marker. This was superior to relying solely on a GPS watch, since invariably—especially in longer distance races like marathons—there was an increasing divergence between the distance as reflected on the mile markers, which were measured based on a perfectly navigated race (known as "running the tangents"), and that shown on your GPS watch. If you followed only your GPS watch for pacing, you would almost certainly miss your goal time as essentially no runner perfectly runs the tangents.

Since I had three goal times, I had to choose which bracelet I wanted to wear. (And no, I never considered wearing three.) I went back and forth before settling on my Plan A time of 4:45, though I worried that if I were wrong about my ability to hit that time, I would be committing the cardinal sin of going out too fast in a marathon. Still, I felt like I could be bold since I had already done the distance once and, of course, the rule about not going out too fast ran headlong into the one that said that you ran your first marathon just to finish and your second for a time. While I had not repeated the mistake of promising Leisha that I would not do another marathon after this one, I expected this would be my last, and I wanted to achieve a PR that would make me proud.

As race day drew closer, I felt a lot better than I had for my first MCM about the amount of my training. I was bothered not to have finished all of it, but drew solace from renowned coach Tom Holland, author of *The Marathon Method*, who argued that you are better off standing at the start of a long race 10% undertrained rather than 1% overtrained. Hopefully I had done enough to achieve my A goal but, at a minimum, to break five hours. I was excited for race morning, repeating everything from two years earlier, right down to the choice of another hoodie for standing in the cold and waiting for the start. I wasn't sure if I would achieve my time goal, but with my Achilles concerns receding, I was at least confident I could cover the distance.

As I stood in the long line of runners waiting for the start, again listening to upbeat music, I took inventory of my gear. I had an audio book queued up—for the 2012 race, I had listened to *Wild* by Cheryl Strayed, which had been perfect: her going on her long journey while I went on mine. For this one, I had chosen another memoir that I thought would be suitable. I moved nicely during the early miles, maintaining a purposefully slower pace than necessary for a 4:45 finish as recommended by Lisa. Holding back was made easier by the thick crowd of slower runners in front of me. In all major marathons, runners are supposed to self-seed based on their anticipated finishing time, using as guides large signs with projected finishing times held aloft in the starting area. Most runners are diligent about this and try to choose accurately. Others position themselves too far forward, either because they misjudge what they are capable of on race day or because they simply want to start closer to the front to increase their chances of making a cut-off. A consequence of these over-ambitious placements is that instead of running in synch with others maintaining a similar pace, you need to pass slower runners. That was my situation now. I was regularly weaving around other racers, with every diversion taking me farther from the tangents. Still, I felt good. The Achilles was holding, it was a beautiful day, and I was confident I could nail my "A" time.

With each passing mile, I checked my pace bracelet. I was playing catch-up because of the slow start but I was steadily improving. The Achilles felt fine, and as the miles went by, I no longer thought about it, exclusively focused on nailing that 4:45 finish. As the last few miles went by, I realized I would easily break 4:50. The only drama now was whether I could get all the way to 4:45. Early in my last mile, my GPS watch beeped, and I looked down. It was alerting me that I had finished the race and easily beaten my goal time. Out on the course, though, I still had nearly a mile to cover. I picked up the pace for the short hill to the Iwo Jima Memorial, the one on which I had been unable to accelerate two years earlier, and crossed the finish line at 4:46:38. According to my watch, I had run 27 miles. All that weaving and my general lack of course discipline had cost me nearly a mile.

Still, I was delighted with the result. I had crushed my prior finish by 35 minutes, easily achieving both my B and C goals and only narrowly missing my A time. Breaking five hours (and, even better, 4:50) seemed more serious, and I loved that I had done two marathons. Now I really did feel like I had done enough, though conscious of the risk that I might one day change my mind again, I kept that thought to myself.

CHAPTER 8

Olympic Distance

By the time I ran my second MCM, I had finished a half dozen or so sprint triathlons. I liked that I had become a triathlete and felt that the races had been successful in giving structure to my daily workouts. I also felt that they helped rather than hindered me professionally, serving both as a welcome distraction from work stresses while, at the same time, helping me keep up with work colleagues who were typically decades younger. I had also been able to structure my daily workouts so that they did not interfere with my parenting responsibilities to our teenage children. Indeed, I felt that they made me a more energetic and positive father.

Even though the races weren't fun, I started to wonder whether I was capable of stepping up to the Olympic distance, roughly twice as long as a sprint. Unlike sprints, Olympic triathlons are standardized: 1. 5-kilometer swim, 40-kilometer bike, and 10K run. (As the name suggests, it is the triathlon distance used for the Olympics.) Having looked at the 10K for so many years as the fitness standard—one that I couldn't meet—I was intrigued at the idea of running a 10K after completing a meaningful swim and bike. By doing that, I thought, I could demonstrate to myself that I had truly been transformed as an athlete. In 2015, I entered the Philadelphia triathlon, and Leisha and I traveled to the city for the Sunday race, where she would later claim third place in her age group for the sprint distance. Unfortunately, the rain picked up in the days leading up to it, and on Saturday they announced the cancellation of the swim. Having already made the trip, I decided to at least get the experience of biking 24. 8 miles—longer than any training ride I had ever attempted—and then running a 10K.

I had purchased an entry-level carbon fiber tri bike a few months earlier, having previously turned in slow performances on a mix of lousy bikes: a mountain bike, a hybrid road/off-road bike, and an old ten-speed that I had gotten in college 35 years earlier. Right away, as the bike leg started, I could tell that this time would be different. I had remembered one sprint tri when I had only passed a single person while being passed by what seemed like 100 or so riders of all ages and shapes. It had been a demoralizing experience. This time I was moving well and passing a bunch of other racers. I would later learn that I had averaged 18.3 mph, more than 3 mph faster than anything I had done before and over a distance that was roughly twice as long as a typical sprint bike leg. The run was even more surprising. I had assumed pre-race that my run leg would be somewhere between an hour and 10 and an hour and 15 minutes. But I did not have any kind of brick feeling in my legs at the start of the run and completed it in just a shade over 59 minutes. This really felt like validation of my fitness progress--not just running a 10K after a nearly 25-mile bike ride but doing it in less than an hour, a barrier that had taken me multiple tries to break at the start of my running journey four years earlier.

Still, I hadn't done a full Olympic tri. I continued to look for one that I could use to scratch the distance off my list. I found a race scheduled for later in the summer on a former military base called Fort Ritchie and signed up. The swim was in a lake and was only my second triathlon swim in open water. My biggest challenge was that I kept pulling to the left and was constantly getting off course, adding unnecessary distance and time. For open water swimming, it is necessary to "sight" (periodically pop your head out of the water and look forward), but I had not practiced it enough. It showed.

The bike leg was challenging. It began with a seven mile downhill, which I knew meant that it would end with seven miles of uphill, and those last miles were every bit as brutal as I had anticipated. That left a two-loop run through the former military base, which was now essentially a ghost town. With the additional exertions of a 1,500-meter swim and a hilly 24.8-mile bike, I had nothing like the energy I had felt in Philadelphia at the start of the run leg. I made my way slowly through the town for my first loop and then repeated it again, with no drama about my ability to finish but also no sense that I was doing it with any kind of style or speed. When I crossed the finish line, I was able mentally to cross off the Olympic distance but without any real enthusiasm or excitement.

I did a second Olympic distance tri at the beginning of the next season. Again, I muddled through and, again, did not enjoy the experience. I realized that when it came to marathons, I did not particularly enjoy the long training runs but found deep meaning and emotional satisfaction in the race itself. With triathlons, it was the opposite. I loved cross-training but did not enjoy the actual race experience. I saw value in continuing with triathlon in order to focus my training but resigned myself to the expectation that I would never find pleasure in the races themselves.

CHAPTER 9

End of the Line

With my Olympic tri experiences having failed to energize me,, I decided to pivot back to the marathon. Maybe I was, after all, a marathoner rather than a triathlete. I entered the 2016 MCM, starting to think that running that race every second year might not be a bad routine. (I was still doing my Arizona commute, which meant 4:30 a.m., mid-week long runs out there.) But with a few months to go before race day, Leisha pointed out that the race conflicted with Parents Weekend at our younger daughter's university, and I had to scramble. I saw that the Philadelphia Marathon was just a few weeks later and signed up for it. That seemed exciting: another big city marathon and a new one at that. Training for Philadelphia went better than it had for either of my two MCMs: no injuries and, finally, a successfully completed 20-mile training run. I assumed I could break five hours again and hoped to do better than I had at the 2014 MCM. I didn't use a coach or do any speed work and felt like showing up at the start line injury-free and having completed all the long runs would be sufficient to turn in a good performance.

Just before the start of the race, I set the distance and time target on my GPS watch for a 4:50 finish. At the expo, I had looked for a racing pace bracelet for this time but had not been able to find one. I got off to a fast start and was about six minutes ahead of my target pace after six miles. I dialed it back but still had a fast first half, beating my half-marathon PR. Though Lisa had recommended a slow start for the MCM that she had coached me through, I didn't mind giving a fast start a try on this day. Ever since my balls-out success at the Home Run 10K, I continued to wonder whether I was leaving something on the table by not pushing myself harder earlier.

The course was very scenic. The first third or so snaked through various parts of the city, including both modern and historical sites. We then spent a long stretch in Fairmount Park. My feelings about the course changed suddenly, though, after mile 16. From there, we ran past the finish line for what was essentially a ten mile out-and-back. This meant that in addition to the frustration of running away from the finish, I now had the demoralizing experience of being confronted by thousands of faster runners who were nearly done while I still had miles to go.

I felt myself progressively slowing over the second half of the race and finished in a little over 4:51. It was nice to break five hours again, but I walked away from the finish area in a negative frame of mind. In addition to the final 10 miles of out and back, the fan support had been considerably less than at MCM. I had not appreciated how truly unique and special that race was. I decided that this was enough marathon running for me. I would, I told myself, be willing to do another with one of my kids if some day they decided it was something they wanted to do and needed company for the effort, but otherwise this time my marathon career had truly come to an end.

I could not see any additional hills to climb as an athlete. On the plus side, I had progressed to the marathon and the Olympic triathlon and was confident in my ability to finish both, something that would have been unthinkable six years earlier when my endurance journey began. But the joy wasn't there now for either type of race. I was committed to fitness, though maybe now it really did just need to be about the workouts.

CHAPTER 10

A Message from Katherine Switzer

A few months after Philadelphia, I saw an article in *The Washington Post* about Katherine Switzer, the first woman to officially run the Boston Marathon. She had done it in 1967 and was now in D.C., getting ready to run in the Cherry Blossom 10-miler in a few days. She would be running the race as part of her training for the Boston Marathon later that month, which, remarkably, she planned to run to celebrate the 50th anniversary of her historic accomplishment.

I had long been an admirer of Switzer and her extraordinary story. The basic outlines of it are now legendary. She was a college student who loved to run and had received special permission to train with her university's men's cross-country team since there was no team for the women. Arnie Briggs, a kind-hearted assistant coach, trained with her, regaling her with stories of the Boston Marathon, a race he had run many times. When Switzer said that she, too, would like to run it, Briggs told her that women were incapable of running marathons. She took that as a challenge. When she had impressed him sufficiently by running the full marathon distance in practice, he agreed to go with her to Boston so that they could run it together.

The race was open to men only, and the prior year a woman had run it as a "bandit" (an unofficial participant who runs without a race number). But Briggs insisted that Switzer officially enter, which she did, using her initials "KV" rather than her first name. She was spotted early in the race, running with Briggs and her boyfriend. Jock Semple, the long-time race director who regarded the Boston marathon as a sacred event, became enraged when he saw Switzer and charged into the crowd of runners. He tried to rip the bib from her sweatshirt, knocking Briggs down in the process. Semple had not reckoned with Switzer's boyfriend, however—a 235-pound collegiate hammer thrower and former football player who threw a shoulder into the race director and sent him flying. The whole sequence was captured in a now iconic series of photographs. Switzer went on to complete the race, surrounded by a protective circle of other runners to prevent any further attempts to forcibly remove her, paving the way a few years later for Boston to finally accept woman racers. (I was touched to read how Switzer and Semple had, in later years, become "the best of friends"—yet a further example of her dignity and courage.)

It was inspiring to see that she was still a terrific runner 50 years after that historic achievement. As I read the story and the recounting of her experience at Boston, she said something unexpected: "One of the races that's always been on my bucket list has been the [56-mile]

Comrades Marathon in South Africa. I've wanted to run that ever since I first heard about it in the late '60s, so who knows, I might get there yet." I, too, had been fascinated by Comrades, a race I had discovered early in my fitness reading. Vic Clapham, a South African veteran of World War I, had started it in 1921 as a living memorial to those of his countrymen who had lost their lives in the Great War. Despite its name, it was an ultra-marathon rather than a standard distance 26.2-mile race. The course was 56 miles long, linking the cities of Pietermaritzburg and Durban. The race snaked through the Valley of a Thousand Hills; only about two kilometers of flat terrain exist along the entire distance. Among the ups and downs, most famous are the big five hills, with the colorful (at least to American ears) names Polly Shorts, Botha's Hill, Inchanga, Fields, and Cowies.

Comrades is known for its unique traditions. The direction of the course alternates each year. The route from Pietermaritzburg to Durban is known as a "down run" because the amount of descending (7,000 feet) exceeds the amount of climbing (5,000 feet). For the "up run" it is, of course, the reverse. The start of the race is marked by the singing of a South African miners' song called *Shosholoza*, described by Nelson Mandela as "a song that compares the apartheid struggle to the motion of an oncoming train." Then there is a recording of *Chariots of Fire*, the most iconic of running songs. And, finally, right before the cannon blast that officially starts the race, there is, of all things, a rooster crow, a tape recording of one that South African

Comrades runner Max Trimborn delivered at the race start over a 32-year period between 1948 and 1980.

There is a strict 12-hour time limit to complete Comrades, with the clock starting the moment the cannon goes off to begin the race, penalizing the unfortunates who start near the back and who may need 10 to 15 minutes just to cross the start line. The race ends inside a stadium, where the last finishers draw the most excitement of the day. This is when the most desperate of the days' participants, some seizing up with cramps and others being dragged along by other runners for the final meters, stagger toward the finish line in the hope of crossing before the cut-off and earning a coveted Comrades medal. An official stands at the finish line, his back to the runners so as not to lose his resolve, and fires a shot at the precise 12-hour mark. At that moment, a phalanx of race officials position themselves across the finish and physically prevent any other runners from crossing.

As I read Switzer's words, it struck me that it was likely too late for her to tackle this particular challenge. At 70, I imagined she was past the age to start training for an ultra like Comrades. (Though if anyone could take on a challenge like Comrades at 70 it would no doubt be Switzer; a few months later she would run her 50th anniversary race in a remarkable 4:44:31.) I was about to turn 55 as I read the article and decided on the spot that I could not let the same thing happen to me. There was still time, I thought, but I would need to start now.

Comrades was still very much in my mind in part because a few years earlier I had started to listen to a podcast called "Run" by a South African running coach named Lindsey Parry. Most of the episodes gave all-purpose running advice. But Lindsey was also the official coach for Comrades, and invariably a great many of his Podcast episodes dealt with questions about the race. I always enjoyed the brief glimpses they provided into what to me was a nearly mythical event. In his unique style, he made the race seem achievable even for runners who might be slower, recovering from injury, undertrained on race day, or facing other setbacks or limitations. Now, I decided, it was time to take Lindsey's words of encouragement to heart.

I concluded that my only chance of finishing the race would be to do the "down" run. While it still had plenty of climbing, and while Lindsey made a good case that the "up" run was easier on the body, for the typical runner the down run can be accomplished at least 10 or so minutes faster. I would need every one of those minutes if I hoped to finish by the cut-off. The race was run on the second Sunday of June, which meant that Comrades 2017 was less than three months away and obviously out of the question. I was pleased to discover that the 2017 race was going to be an up run, which meant that 2018 would be down and, therefore, the one for me.

I started to research the practical logistics of entering. Would-be-entrants had to qualify, which at that time meant running a marathon in less than five hours. The precise time mattered; runners were organized into different "batches" on race day. Faster qualifying times placed runners in batches closer to the start, with the fastest runners in batch A and the slowest in batch H. It was those slowest runners in batch H, the ones most at risk of missing the 12-hour cut-off, who could count on losing 10-15 minutes at the start of the race as they slowly moved toward the start line. Clearly, I would be a batch H runner. The Comrades website also included training plans for runners of various skill levels. I studied the plan for the slowest runners, those who were just looking to finish the race before the final gun—the "finisher's" plan. Other than the qualifying marathon, which could be run at any time between September and May, the finisher's plan called for two more marathons and a 50K, all run at approximately 4-week intervals between March and May. That seemed daunting. I had always thought of marathons as, at best, a once-a-year activity or, in my case, once every two years.

The finisher's plan also contemplated four runs per week, with long runs on back-to-back days. These are known among ultra runners as "sandwich" runs. They force runners to do their longest run of the week on slightly tired legs from the day before. Pretty much everything I had ever read about running for older runners who were looking to have a long career in the sport stressed the importance of cross-training and advised against running two days in a row. But it was clear that I would have to embrace sandwich runs despite all of this. If nothing else, I knew intuitively that my only chance of finishing was to do precisely what the plan told me.

Nearly all runners get injured at some point, and injuries had certainly been a regular feature of my running experience. It is simply a part of the sport. Learning to recognize that an injury is beginning and adjusting training to prevent it from developing further—what coaches refer to as "listening to your body"— is as critical a running skill as any. Still, for this race, I decided to be more proactive. I went to see Rachel Miller, an outstanding physical therapist who had treated me following several of my prior injuries. I explained my plan to run Comrades and told her that I wanted to get out ahead of things and do everything I could to bullet-proof my body against injury. Rachel gave me a series of hip exercises, an area of weakness that she had previously identified. She also suggested that I try to make my Comrades qualifier early to give myself maximum time to recover before the race itself, which would also help reduce injury risk. Rachel told me about an October marathon in Pennsylvania called Steamtown, a point-to-point race with a lot of downhills that was popular with runners in the area who were looking for a fast course to improve their chances of qualifying for the Boston marathon. I went ahead and signed up for it, excited that my Comrades plan was starting to take shape.

CHAPTER 11

The Road to Comrades

I planned on once again running the Parks half marathon in September as part of my training for Steamtown. My training was going well, but one thing kept bothering me: my toes really suffered on longer runs. My shoes seemed to be the right size, yet the toes still hurt. I wondered if a switch to a shoe with a larger toe box would help. I went to a local running store with a great reputation and got fitted for a different style shoe that felt right. I started training with the new shoes. For a few weeks, everything went well. Then, on a longer run, I felt pain in my hip. Within a few days, it was clear that it wasn't a fluke. I was again injured. I ditched the new shoes and went for physical therapy.

Over a period of weeks, I tried to resume training, but each time the pain returned. The half-marathon was getting closer—and, beyond that, Steamtown—yet I still couldn't get back on track. Desperate to resume training, I decided to give Jeff Galloway's run-walk strategy a proper try. I knew I would need to use run-walk for Comrades, anyway—everyone except the elites did that—so I had no reason not to start experimenting with it now. Over the next few weeks as I resumed my training for Parks, I experimented with various combinations and finally settled on 5 minutes/1 minute, reconciled to staying with run/walk for the foreseeable future. I would be slower, but at least I was running again. I built my distance back up, and as race day approached, I was confident that I could finish.

The race started and I headed out with the intention of strictly following my run/walk plan. In what seemed like too short a period of time, I received an alert on my Garmin for my first walk break. I felt awkward doing it, with so many runners around and right at the beginning of the race, but I was committed. The route through the park system was as pleasant as I remembered, and the weather was in the 50s—perfect for racing. I settled into a rhythm and, without a specific time goal, tried to just enjoy the race.

I felt strong right from the beginning but did not check my time for the first 10 miles. At the 10-mile mark I finally looked at my watch and saw that I was at a little over 1:44. Though I hadn't set a time goal, in a prior attempt at Parks I had tried and failed to break 2:20. With only three miles to go and given my pace to that point, I realized that I would for sure break 2:20 and even had a shot at 2:15 if I really turned it on. I decided to go for it. As I crossed the finish line, I looked down at my Garmin. It read 2:14:32. I had broken 2:15 and had dropped my PR by almost seven minutes. And, with that, I was sold on run-walk, not just as a post-injury training strategy but as one that I could confidently rely on for speed in longer races.

I experienced some soreness, but the intense hip pain had not returned. Ecstatic over the time and while still in the finisher's area, I searched for a finishing-time predictor and entered 2:14:32, looking to see what it calculated for the marathon. It predicted 4:40:30. I didn't intend to be that aggressive at Steamtown, but it gave me confidence that I could easily hit the 5:00 qualifying time and that I had a good shot at breaking 4:45 and getting a new PR.

My training continued without incident after Parks, the hip injury a receding memory and sore toes now an accepted part of my running, moderated ever so slightly by the use of thinner socks. (It would be several more years until finally, on the advice of a coach, I moved up a half-size while staying with the same shoe model, which solved my remaining toe pain issues.) As the race drew nearer, I had a new concern: weather. One of the reasons I had chosen Steamtown was that the timing of the race typically meant cooler fall temperatures. Yet, when I started checking the long-range weather forecast on my phone, it kept showing the low temperature for the day in the 70s. Temperatures in the 70s and above can trim 10% or even more off running speed from back-of-the-packers like me. I kept expecting the forecast to change as the race got closer, but it didn't. On race morning, I caught sight of an illuminated sign in front of a bank that alternated between showing the time of day and the temperature. At 6:05 a.m., it was 75. My phone told me that the high around the time I expected to finish would be 78.

The race started near a local high school. It was clear that this was going to be very different from the big city marathons I had run. It had a sweet, small-town feel. There was even a squad of high school cheerleaders on hand to add a celebratory spirit to the start. Once underway, I settled into a rhythm. The course profile called for significant downhill from mile 3 to mile 8, followed by milder downhills all the way out to mile 24. Then, over the last two miles, three uphill segments awaited, the most challenging part of the otherwise runner-friendly course. But it was getting hot, and by mile 9, I had finished the 20-ounce bottle of Gatorade that I was carrying on a hydration belt. The next aid station was nowhere in sight. Panic started to creep in. I didn't see how I could stay sufficiently hydrated over the rest of the race, which would be disastrous for my time. And then—salvation. Someone had set up their own unofficial aid station with bottles of water, and I grabbed one. I would encounter two more of these in later miles, something I had never seen before. I was able to keep going and even, for the first 16 miles, at a sub-4:45 pace.

After that, I could feel myself slow down, and I had to admit that a new PR was out of the question. But with the Comrades qualifying requirement at 5:00, I felt like I had plenty of cushion. And then, at mile 19, I felt my right hamstring starting to cramp, a definite sign that I was getting dehydrated despite the extra water bottles. At mile 22 disaster struck. The hamstring completely seized up. For an instant, I could not continue forward at all. I pulled my right heel to my butt. It wasn't a hamstring stretch, but for whatever reason, the spasm seemed to lessen. After a few tentative steps I resumed running. The hamstring calmed down, but I was thoroughly rattled, expecting a recurrence at any moment. I ticked off the last few miles and crossed the finish line in slightly less than 4:55, so depleted from the effort that I had to lay down on a nearby patch of grass immediately after getting my finishers medal. At least I had qualified.

CHAPTER 12

The BHAG

Comrades was very obviously a "reach" goal for me. I analogized it to what Jim Collins, author of the classic business book *Good to Great*, had written about companies that had successfully separated themselves from their competitors and become industry leaders. (I had read the book as part of my introduction to the business world after beginning my new job in Arizona where, as a company, we were very focused on becoming "great" and, indeed, would become one of the industry's top performers.) Companies that had made the transition from "good" to "great" had, based on Collins' research, done so by consciously defining and pursuing that outcome in the form of a "big hairy audacious goal" or "BHAG." He defined a BHAG as "a powerful way to stimulate progress." To do so, the goal must be "clear and compelling." Collins gives the example of John F. Kennedy's goal of landing men on the moon by the end of the 1960s, which required "both building for the long term AND exuding a relentless sense of urgency." A BHAG had to be the right amount of difficult. According to Collins, it "should fall well outside the comfort zone" and, while there should be a basis for believing it can be achieved, it "should require heroic effort and perhaps even a little luck."

I decided that the BHAG concept could apply on a personal level as well, leading an individual on their own "good to great" journey, in my case taking me from being an ordinary middle-aged runner to becoming someone who had successfully tackled one of the world's greatest ultramarathons. As it does for a company, I felt that a personal BHAG can have an energizing, focusing effect through the invariable ups and downs while chasing a challenging and exciting goal. Of course, it would have to be "audacious," which meant that it had to be in that band between what was almost certainly achievable with focused effort and what was truly out of reach. To me, Comrades fell perfectly into that zone.

But the very real chance of failure also caused me to think more specifically about my plans for after the race. I had read about the depression that many runners experience in the immediate aftermath of achieving a big goal. Once the initial excitement of crossing the finish line passes, a feeling of loss arises after realizing that the goal is now in the past. It's a cliché, but so much of the joy in anything, including distance running, is in the journey rather than the destination. Endurance sports writers have not just identified the problem but also suggested a solution: pick out your next goal *before* you tackle your upcoming milestone race. That way, the moment you cross the finish line, you can re-focus on the next big thing. If achieving a major goal could be followed by post-race depression, I had to assume that the emotional toll would be far greater from failing to cross the finish line. I therefore decided that I really needed to focus on what would follow Comrades.

A few years earlier, shortly before going to bed, I had spent a few minutes examining my running/triathlon career to that point, typing my thoughts into an iPad, and wondered what I might be able to achieve in the future. I decided that a half-Ironman (1.2-mile swim, 56-mile bike, and half marathon) might be theoretically possible, even though the bike and running portions would each be more than double those of an Olympic distance tri. I completely ruled out the possibility of ever doing a full Ironman (2.4-mile swim, 112-mile bike, and full marathon). As I wrestled with what to do after Comrades, I thought back to that exercise. I decided to go for a half-Ironman the year following Comrades. And then, the summer after that, I would go even further. I would follow the Comrades BHAG with a second one: Ironman.

CHAPTER 13

No Turning Back

However gruesome Steamtown had been, at least the business of qualifying for Comrades was behind me. The finisher's plan did not begin until January, so I continued with my usual training schedule (three days running, two days biking, one day swimming) for the next few months. I knew the sandwich runs were coming and was reconciled to doing them, but I saw no need to get started early. A particular malady affecting Comrades runners is to overdo things on the classic theory that if some is good, more is better, but Lindsey Parry had always admonished against that kind of thinking. I didn't need any convincing. I was too conscious of my history of running injuries to want to expose myself any earlier than necessary to the risk of getting hurt again.

As January approached, I studied the finisher's plan constantly. It was intense. Given my injury history, which had affected my preparation for three of the four marathons I had run, I thought there was an excellent chance that I would never make it to the start line. Those injuries had come on a 3-day-a-week running schedule. Now I would be running four days a week, with back-to-back long runs, which clearly increased my risk. Still, I had committed myself to this challenge and was determined to move forward. I knew that I needed to focus on only the week ahead and not get overwhelmed by the intense training later in the plan. Another Comrades tradition is to give each year's race a unique Zulu name. The name for Comrades 2018 was Asijiki, "No Turning Back," which fit my attitude perfectly as I got underway.

As January began, I started ticking off the workouts. I printed out the plan and attached it to a clipboard, putting an X through each run as I completed it. The month came and went without any drama as far as my training was concerned. A seismic event shook my personal life, though. I separated from Leisha after 25 years of marriage and moved from the D. C. area to New York. (The prior year my office had moved from Scottsdale, Arizona to Manhattan, and I had been commuting to there several days each week.) Leisha and I had been together for five years before getting married, which meant that we had been a couple for more than half of my life. The mutual unhappiness, and several unsuccessful attempts to address it with couples therapy, had begun years prior to my foray into endurance sports. Learning to live apart from her and navigating the adjustment with our four adult children were going to be huge emotional challenges.

The change did not interfere with my training, however. I found the attention that Comrades prep demanded to be a welcome distraction from all that came with going through a divorce. In times of stress, I could always shift my focus to Comrades. In some ways, distance racing had always been an escape from life's myriad pressures for me. It was also more than that. Putting in the effort and making sacrifices, sometimes painful ones, in the pursuit of a goal was truly a metaphor for life, perhaps never more appropriately than at this time. I knew the divorce was necessary and was confident that we would both be in a better place once the process had run its course and we were on the other side. But getting there was going to be challenging and fraught with emotional cost. I needed to accept that and continue to move forward.

I made my way through February, pleasantly surprised to be running four days a week without incident. The first Sunday in March called for a "training marathon," an amusing phrase that I had never heard prior to beginning my Comrades journey. I found it remarkable that a marathon could just be training for something longer, rather than a milestone event in its own right. But it also felt right. If I truly wanted to have a chance to finish a race that was 30 miles longer than a marathon, I needed to start to cultivate a more casual, matter-of-fact attitude toward the 26.2-mile distance.

In Rhode Island, I found a small-town race called the Oceans Marathon. I ran it without any drama at a slow pace, with a time of slightly more than 5:21. I was fine with the time. I had been focused on completing the distance rather than running it for speed. When it was done, I did not feel wrecked or exhausted, but it was hard to imagine running

4.8 miles farther for a 50K in another month. Doing more than double the distance for Comrades was something that I still couldn't get my head around.

CHAPTER 14

Going Beyond 26.2

After a 1-week reverse taper that included a Sunday long run of just one hour, the training pace picked back up again. Two weeks after the Oceans Marathon, my long run was three hours, which followed a 1 hour 45-minute run the day before. The following week my weekend runs were 2 hours/3 hours 30 minutes. And then, only one month removed from Oceans, I was again into a single week taper. But this next race would be different. It would be a 50K, my first ultra.

50K races are harder to find than marathons for the simple reason that they are not very popular. Far fewer people run them. Early in my running journey a friend who ran ultras shared with me his favorite running quote: "Any idiot can run a marathon, but it takes a special kind of idiot to run an ultra." After some searching, I was able to locate one in nearby Delaware: the Trap Pond 50K. The course map called for a short out and back run of about 2.5 miles, followed by six loops of slightly under five miles each on a forest trail around a lake. The race also had a marathon option and those running 26.2 miles would do five loops. As the race approached, I wondered what the start of that final loop would feel like, knowing that those doing the marathon would already be done while I still had a fair amount of running to do. I also had misgivings about the loop concept generally. I was worried that the repetition might be maddening.

The start was a decidedly casual affair, just a bunch of us gathered around a small start area and then heading out when the race director told us it was time. After the short out and back, we settled in for the first loop. Very quickly I decided I really liked the course. The trail was firmly packed and smooth, with just the occasional pinecone or stick to avoid. The lake was beautiful, particularly as the sun began to rise. And it was all so peaceful—running in the woods with almost no one around. It was, I recognized, one of those unique experiences that makes distance running so special.

As I approached the end of the 5th loop, I realized that I didn't mind the prospect of going back out. It had all been so relaxed: the comfortable trail, the beautiful sunrise over the lake, and the solitude and quiet. As I proceeded along my 6th loop, delighted that each step represented a new personal distance record, I noticed a small crack in the feelings of strength and control that I had been able to maintain up to that point. My right quad started to quiver as though it was about to go into a full spasm. Fortunately, I was able to complete the loop without incident.

I crossed the finish line excited to have completed my first ultra. It had been a terrific confidence booster. My pacing was still a problem, though. Looking over the data from my Garmin, I saw that I had gotten progressively slower over each of the last three loops, with the final one being over 13 minutes a mile, which was obviously not going to work for Comrades. This was despite the fact that it would have been hard to imagine a more runner-friendly course profile, completely unlike what I would experience in the hills of South Africa.

With the 50K behind me, I was still in early April, with the biggest sandwiches of the training schedule waiting for me at the end of the month. Prior to beginning the training plan, this was the month that I expected to challenge me the most, with the greatest chance of an injury that would derail the whole effort. The runs for that first April weekend went well, the first a scenic run down the Hudson River, then looping around lower Manhattan and running along the East River before turning around. I covered nearly 22 miles on the Sunday run following the same route, my longest training run (excluding the Oceans "training" marathon) ever. I had felt surprisingly good. I had slowed somewhat later in the run, but not that much. The next weekend went even better. For the Sunday run, I was able to maintain an almost even pace throughout the nearly 24 miles that I covered. It was exciting to realize that the increase in training load was not tearing my body down. Instead, my strength and speed kept improving throughout the month—not at all as I had imagined it before January. That, of course, was the inherent logic of the plan. Understanding it was one thing; physically experiencing it was pleasantly different.

May promised to be a generally lighter month though I had to figure out the first Sunday. The training plan had the following intriguing entry: "REST or 50-55 km Long Run." Resting was, of course, the attractive option, especially after two consecutive weeks that featured long runs of over 21 miles. But as I listened to more of Lindsey Parry's podcasts, it became clear that there really wasn't a choice. What was known as the "Comrades long run"—a training run of at least 50 km, preferably occurring exactly five weeks before race day, was considered essential. Much as I craved taking it easy for a single weekend, I knew I had to find another 50K.

I searched extensively but could not find another official race of that distance for the Sunday that I needed it. In South Africa, runners typically do the Comrades long run with their running club—no one wants to do it by themselves if they can avoid it—but a running club was not an option for me. The next best thing would be to find a marathon and simply tack on 4.8 miles to make my own 50K. That way I would at least have the company of other runners and aid stations for most of the run, to be preceded or followed by slightly less than an hour of solitary effort.

I found a marathon in Providence, Rhode Island that worked with my schedule. The course design looked to be fairly interesting, with much of it along a river. Having chosen the race, I was left with one big decision: when to tack on the extra miles. Doing it pre-race would allow me to finish with other runners and head right over to grab some post-race refreshments. But to really feel like I had run a single 50K rather than a marathon and a separate

4.8-mile training run in the same morning, I would need to plan the completion of that short segment so that I arrived at the start area within a few minutes of the beginning of the race. I couldn't cut it too close. Arriving after all the runners had already headed out on the course sounded like the plot of a pre-race anxiety dream. The alternative was to add the extra miles post-race, which would mean blasting through the finish area and continuing on, finisher's medal in hand, to cover the additional distance. I decided on the pre-race option.

On race morning, I left my hotel at 5:30 a.m. to have enough time to drive to packet pick-up for my race bib and then run 4.8 miles before the start of the race, but I hadn't counted on all the race-related road closures. I eventually had to drive back to my hotel, drop off my car, and walk to packet pick-up. That left me with only enough time to do 3.8 miles before the start, meaning that my extra miles would involve both pre- and post-race segments. The logistics of the first segment went off without a hitch. I completed the short run and arrived back at the starting area with four minutes to spare, just enough time to jump into a porta potty, with the national anthem finishing as I walked out.

The main part of my day's run—the actual marathon—ended up being straightforward. As I approached the finish line, I slowed only enough to grab a finisher's medal and a water bottle and then kept right on going. When I later looked over my Garmin data for the day, I saw that my splits, while not yet negative, were improved over Oceans and Trap Pond. I was making progress.

CHAPTER 15

The Spirit of Comrades

With Providence done, the final daunting part of my training plan was behind me. In just two months—from the beginning of March to the beginning of May—I had run a marathon; a 50K; the 50K Comrades long run; and had also completed my two longest training runs of the program, each of which had gone over 21 miles. Two weeks after Providence, I had my final long weekend running of two hours/three hours, and then I was into the taper. Before I had started, I figured I probably had less than a 50% chance of even getting to the start line. Yet, here I was, uninjured and with the training in my rearview mirror.

I turned my attention to the logistical details involved with the race. Even though the down run started in Pietermaritzburg, most runners stayed in Durban where it would finish. Durban is a coastal city on the Indian Ocean with plenty of hotels, while Pietermaritzburg is inland and much less of a tourist destination. A Durban stay also meant a short trip to the hotel after finishing instead of a long, uncomfortable bus ride after 12 hours of racing. The flip side, of course, was the need for an early morning trip to Pietermaritzburg on race day. With a 5:30 am race start, that would not leave much time for sleep.

Getting to Durban from New York was a 3-flight odyssey: New York to London, London to Johannesburg, and Johannesburg to Durban. I got into Durban Thursday afternoon before the race, checking into the hotel before dinner. There I met up with my youngest brother Josh, nearly 20 years my junior. Josh loved to travel and was planning on combining his trip to see me with some extended sightseeing in the rest of the country. I joked with people that he was there to claim the body if things didn't go well. Josh was a good sport, patiently listening to me drone on about the race and its history. He joined me for a 20-minute run through the streets of Durban, the very last X on my training plan.

There was an event late that afternoon for the international runners, and I was looking forward to meeting other people on this same adventure. Training for Comrades in the States is a lonely pursuit. To now be surrounded by so many others who really got it made up for the long, solitary months of training. But the thing that I was most looking forward to was the chance to meet Bruce Fordyce, the legendary "King of Comrades." Fordyce had won the race an astonishing nine times between 1981 and 1990.

Fordyce spoke to our group about the "Spirit of Comrades," a combination of camaraderie, selflessness, dedication, perseverance, and humanity. One way that spirit had expressed itself over the years was the tradition of runners physically helping someone who might be in a state of almost complete physical collapse within yards of the finish line, dragging or carrying the stricken runner while imperiling their own ability to finish before the cut-off. Fordyce also had some tips for the race. Among other things, he cautioned us slower runners in H Batch that we could expect to lose 15 minutes before crossing the start line. I struggled to believe that it could really be that bad. Afterward, I was thrilled to be able to go up and get a picture with him.

The next day it was time for another Comrades tradition: the pre-race bus tour, a chance for the first-timers to see the entire course. I had mixed feelings about signing up for it. I had read a story about some guy who had taken the tour and, when it was over, packed up and left South Africa, wanting no part of the course once he had seen it. I had never previously scouted a course, so it was certainly not part of some pre-race ritual for me. Still, this race was obviously going to be different, so Josh and I dutifully took the trip. As the bus moved along, alternately climbing and descending, I couldn't decide if I was intimidated or reassured, but I certainly didn't feel panicked. It would be a hell of a day, but it didn't seem impossible.

With the bus tour behind us, Josh and I went to the expo so that I could pick up my race bib and buy some Comrades-themed souvenirs. One of the race-day questions I had long struggled with was whether to join a "bus." That's the South African name for a group that runs with a pace leader. There would be two 12-hour buses, the goal of which was to get runners across the finish line minutes before the cut-off. It was tempting. In theory you simply climbed aboard at the beginning and held on for dear life, leaving to the "bus driver" the mental strain of deciding proper pacing for the different sections of the course. But the challenge was that if the driver had a different run-walk strategy than you had trained with, running with a bus could easily destroy your race. Lindsey and most other coaches thought it best to avoid the buses, with the qualification that jumping on one for the final few kilometers might be *the* thing that could help you make it across. That advice seemed sound to me, but I was still intrigued. The various bus drivers were gathered at the Expo, and I chatted with the two who were going to lead the 12-hour groups. Neither was planning on my precise run-walk ratio, and, for me, that was that.

Without the ability to rely on an experienced bus driver, I had to come up with my own race strategy. I found some pace charts on a Facebook post. There was one that targeted, precisely, a 12-hour finish, which seemed terrifying. To run an entire day knowing that a mistake of a single minute would doom your race struck me as a prescription for extended mental torture. An 11:40 plan, on the other hand, seemed too aggressive and would have me go out too fast in the first half, only to blow up in the second. I thought an 11:50 plan struck the right balance. Choosing a target finish time was only part of the race strategy process. The pace charts also accounted for splits—positive, negative or even. Given my track record in marathons and the 50K distances I had run, I chose a chart that contemplated a slight positive split – completing the first half in 5:52:30 (12:42 minutes per mile) and the second in 5:57:30 (12:47 minutes per mile).

The night before the race promised to be stressful. The general rule among distance runners is that you really want to get a good night's sleep two nights before a big race, on the assumption that you will not sleep well the last night because of pre-race jitters. But with 12 hours of running ahead of me, the idea of only getting a couple of hours sleep the night before the race seemed like a recipe for disaster. I was desperately hoping to do better than that. A complicating factor—on top of the long distance to Pietermaritzburg and the early hour of the start—was an announcement that there was road construction and that it would be best to take one of the earlier buses to avoid a delay that might cause you to miss the start of the race. I hadn't come this far to lose everything in a traffic jam and decided to get on one of the very first buses, which would start pulling out of Durban at 1:30 a.m.

I had all my stuff laid out in the hotel room by 9 p.m. and got into bed, hoping to get four good hours of sleep before I would need to get up and head to the buses. I thought about taking a Benadryl to help ensure that I would fall asleep but worried that I would wake up drowsy and decided not to. That was a mistake. I must have slept a few minutes here and there, but it seemed like I tossed and turned the entire time. Shortly after 1 a.m., completely awake, I got out of bed as scheduled, gathered my things, and headed out into the darkness, the biggest day of my running life about to begin.

CHAPTER 16

Shosholoza

Shortly before 1:45 I boarded the very first bus. I knew I would avoid traffic jams but also had probably taken it a bit too far. I tried to rationalize my decision, hoping that if nothing else, it would allow me to grab a spot near the front of H Batch, which might allow me to shave a few minutes off the long trudge toward the start line after the cannon went off. The bus arrived in Pietermaritzburg with no drama. As planned, I headed right for the front of H, sitting on the ground as the other runners around me were also doing. I had on a hoodie, gloves, and pair of sweatpants, but I still found the 40-degree cold somewhat bracing.

In reading Comrades race reports, I had learned of the practice of some runners to write a mantra or something else that might inspire them when things got tough later in the race. I was wearing a plastic bracelet that was my ticket for the bus and decided to write some initials on it that might serve that purpose. I decided on two: TYT and BOT.

The first stood for "trust your training." I had done essentially every single workout on the finishers plan, and

I needed to trust that it would be enough to get me to the stadium in less than 12 hours regardless of any doubts that might enter my head as the hours ticked by and the fatigue and pain of such a long race increased. The other one, BOT, stood for "break on through"— actually for "break on through to the other side." It was inspired, of course, by the Doors song of that name. In my mind, Comrades loomed as a kind of epic challenge that stood between where I currently was in life—essentially an ordinary back-of-the-pack runner with a few marathons under his belt—and the glory of achieving an extraordinary athletic challenge that few would dare to try. The day would be brutal, but if I could somehow make it, I would find myself in a different emotional place, having just accomplished something life-altering.

I had gotten seated in the pen starting around 3 a. m., two and a half hours before the start. I saw others shift to standing, and it soon became clear that standing was better than sitting because of the cold. At about five, I took off my pants and stuffed them in the string backpack I was wearing, wondering how I was going to get rid of it since I was in the middle of the road, with crowds of runners on either side of me. Then, I thought about my phone. One of Comrades' unfortunate traditions was that it still prohibited the wearing of headphones. The idea that I would need to be in my own head, with no distractions, for 12 hours of running seemed, in some ways, almost as daunting as the physical challenge of completing the distance. At the same time, the Comrades app had a feature that allowed people to track your position throughout the race using your cell phone signal. That meant that you needed to carry your phone with you so that you could be tracked. I took off one of my gloves and shoved it in my hoodie pocket so that I could access the app and make sure that everything was set for tracking. I had told my kids about the tracking feature and wanted to make sure they would be able to monitor my progress.

At around 5:15, the barriers separating the batches were dropped, and everybody moved slightly forward. A couple of minutes later, the traditional Comrades starting rituals began. First, it was the South African national anthem, sung in an astonishing five different languages. After that, it was *Shosholoza*. On the bus tour, they had handed out a song sheet with the lyrics, which were a mix of words from two local languages, Zulu and Ndebele. I tried to commit them to memory; I really wanted to participate fully in the singing. Try as I might, though, I just couldn't get down much beyond the word *Shosholoza* itself, which fortunately was repeated throughout the song. I didn't feel too badly about it though. When Bruce Fordyce had spoken a few nights earlier, he had teased all of us who were trying to learn *Shosholoza*, admitting that despite all the Comrades races he had run (29 in total, including his 9 victories), he had never mastered the words.

I looked around at the tightly packed sea of runners singing. Being in the middle of it was immensely powerful. It was still dark, and searchlights danced off the buildings—all in all, a dazzling, moving experience. After *Shosholoza*, it was, as expected, *Chariots of Fire*, the ultimate running soundtrack. I strained my ears for what was to come next, and then, sure enough, I could clearly hear the rooster crow. A moment after that, there was the boom of a cannon, and the race was officially underway.

I started my Garmin, but, of course, in a physical sense the race had only really begun for those in A batch, who were now surging past the start line. (While virtually every other race effectively equalizes the start time for all participants by beginning the clock when a timing mat at the start line is crossed, Comrades tradition mandated a single start time for everyone.) For us H batchers, the trudging continued, the minutes ticking by. Finally, after nearly 10 minutes of walking, I could see the start. I also picked out, just before that, a fenced enclosure in the very middle of the road that runners had to move around. I quickly took off the backpack with my sweatpants inside, bunched it up with my hoodie, and threw both over the fence as I passed by the enclosure. I intended to hang on to the gloves. It was still in the 40s, and I would want them for the next few hours until the temperature rose. But a moment too late, I realized I had never put back on the glove that I had taken off to use my phone. It had gone over the fence, still stuffed in the pocket of my hoodie.

Moments later we were across the start line. A quick glance down at my watch showed that ten minutes and 46 seconds had elapsed. I was actually thrilled. Bruce Fordyce had told us H batchers to expect to lose 15 minutes, and in my mind, I had just banked four precious minutes at the very beginning of the race. In planning for race day, I always knew that every minute would count. Lindsey Parry had a formula for predicting how much time it should take to run Comrades. It required you to take your marathon time and multiple it by 2.5. Based on that formula, my 4:55 qualifying time predicted a 12:17 finish. Since the cut-off would be 12 hours, the math didn't work for the slower runners like me. We would have to outperform the formula on race day. And, of course, the time limit wasn't really 12 hours for anyone who wasn't standing right next to the start line when the cannon was fired. Based on when I crossed the start line, the cut-off would be 11:49:14, meaning that I needed to exceed my predicted finish time by nearly 30 minutes. This was a huge part of the dilemma for those of us in H. The racers in the early pens, through F, statistically were able to finish at well over a 90% rate. But for G batch, the figure was 60%, and for H batch it dropped to 50%. That percentage—representing a one-in-two chance of finishing—haunted me. I had never started a race, except perhaps for my first Marine Corps marathon where I had been battling a knee injury, with doubt about whether I would be able to finish within the allotted time.

So, where was that time going to come from? On one of his podcasts, Lindsey talked about how to save 20 minutes on race day. Primarily, this involved one rule: "I will not stop." That meant that at aid stations—there would be 40 of them—you needed to keep moving while you took what you needed. Coming to a full stop would cost you 30 seconds, and if you did that at half of the aid stations, which would be 10 minutes lost right there. You should also not stop by the side of the road for a quick leg massage offered by student physical therapists to aching runners. The only exception to the "don't stop" rule should be to use a toilet.

Lindsey's tips might net me somewhere between 10 and 20 minutes, but I still needed to find other savings. Another way was to improve my pace for the walk breaks. I was a naturally slow walker, a subject of frequent teasing by my younger daughter Tali, a college sophomore who had stayed with me in Manhattan for the summer. I knew that I needed to change that. In the last couple of months before the race, I had set out to consciously work on my walking speed, turning my feet over faster and pumping my arms back and forth with a sense of purpose. Judging by my Garmin, my walking pace improved from over 17 minutes per mile to around 15. If I ended up walking about one-sixth of the race, that would translate into nearly two hours of walking. A savings of 2 minutes-per-mile over that distance would give me an additional 15 or so minutes of benefit.

The final area I had focused on was weight. For that there is a formula: every extra pound you carry can cost you two seconds per mile in running pace. That may not sound like much, but in a nearly 60-mile race, it meant that every extra pound would translate into 2 minutes lost on race day. In a race in which every minute counted, these were important numbers. A 5-pound loss could mean fully 10 minutes of savings. I had done well with this, taking my weight from 202 in January to 190 before I got on the plane in New York for the trip to South Africa.

Those were my Comrades "hacks." I hoped that, together, they would get me across the finish line within the time I had to work with. In the hours-long wait for the race to begin, I had thought about all of them. In theory, at least, I felt like I had done enough to find 30 minutes or so in savings. Still, I couldn't entirely push away the negative thoughts. My longest run had been less than 6 and a half hours, and now I would need to exceed that by nearly another five and half hours. Was I really ready for this?

CHAPTER 17

Cut-Offs

When I had first thought about Comrades and the challenge of successfully completing the race, my focus had always been the strict, 12-hour limit for finishing. But as I got more deeply into things, I learned that the finish line was essentially the last of seven cut-offs that runners had to cross by specific times during the race. The others were Lion Park (15.57km), Cato Ridge (30.28km), Drummond (44.27km), Winston Park (57.61km), Pinetown (68.86km), and Sherwood (80.88km). They were spaced anywhere from 11 to 15 km apart, with Lion Park needing to be crossed within 2 hours and 30 minutes and Sherwood, the last of the pre-stadium cut-offs, by the race's 11-hour mark. Anyone failing to reach a cut-off within the allotted time would be stopped, put onto a "bailer bus," and taken to the stadium.

There was a school of thought among experienced Comrades runners that the cut-offs should be used to "chunk" the race into manageable segments. If you thought of the race not as a single, daunting, 90-kilometer ultra but instead as seven individual runs of between 11 and 15 kilometers, all your running that day would be in pursuit of something that was quite manageable, shorter even than a half-marathon. I liked that strategy although, of course, it would require immense mental discipline to block out the segments still to come. Whether you chunked the race or not, slower runners like me needed to be mindful of the cut-offs. I laminated a small piece of paper with the names and times and carried it with me so that I would be able to regularly monitor my progress.

It was still cold and dark as we moved out of Pietermaritzburg, and I was missing the second glove. Every few minutes my uncovered hand would become numb, and I switched the remaining glove back-and-forth until, finally, it was warm enough that I didn't need it anymore. It was soon clear that I was nicely on track for the first cut off and, for better or worse, ahead of schedule as I passed it with more than 20 minutes to spare. For the first 20 or so kilometers, I was doing well with a 5-minute/1 minute run-walk ratio, with a few extra walks for some of the uphill portions and a few skipped breaks for some of the long downhills. Soon after, I began to feel a bit tired and sweaty. For the first time since the start, I began to wonder whether I would have enough in the tank to cover the entire distance still ahead of me. I tried to block out those thoughts.

Another unique aspect of Comrades is the way that progress is marked on the course. The markers are, of course, in kilometers rather than miles, but the unusual thing is that they count down rather than up. The first one we saw that morning was 89, and after 20 km of running they had dipped below 70. Judging from race reports, many runners found it demoralizing to be so specifically confronted with the enormous amount of running still ahead. I found that I liked seeing the numbers going down, and each time a new tens digit appeared—from 80 to 70, 70 to 60, etc.— I felt a small surge of accomplishment. It struck me as the markers were approaching 60 that I was nearly a third of the way through the race, and that was encouraging.

But not long after passing the second cut-off and completing the first 30 km, the first problems appeared. My right leg started spasming, both in the hamstring and in the calf. I decided to start varying my run-walk ratio, trying all sorts of different combinations to deal with the problem. I also started taking salt. As I worked on sorting out the spasms, I was at least able to keep moving forward.

My other preoccupation related to my nutrition. The aid stations provided water, an energy drink called Energade, and Coke. I started the day mostly drinking Energade, and then, when the spasms began, I switched to Coke. Through much of my 30s, I had been a big Coke drinker, often going through an entire six-pack in a day. I had finally stopped drinking soda altogether nearly 20 years earlier, but finisher reports about the miraculous, restorative power of Coke on Comrades race day had led me to try it a few times during training, and it really did seem to help.

Whatever impact the Coke might be having on my leg issues, after a few hours of running I started to get nervous that I might be dehydrated. I had peed a couple of times early in the race, but then hour after hour felt no need to pee again, which was never how I felt in marathons. I made a conscious effort to hydrate more and in addition to the Coke, started also drinking water. For food, I was carrying a half-dozen gels and also had arranged for three bag drops along the route with a local company called Consports. As the day progressed, I realized that I was not hungry at all. The gels were the only thing that I felt like eating. I tried a few bites of banana at one aid station, a section of orange at another, and a peanut butter and jelly sandwich from a drop bag, but none of it was appealing. This was completely unlike my experience at the Trap Pond 50K, where I had feasted throughout the race. I did not think I could run for 12 hours on gels alone, but forcing down unappetizing food was not a realistic option, either.

Despite the distractions over the spasms, the need to constantly vary my run-walk times, and concern over my food and hydration, I continued to move forward. As I came closer to the third cut-off at Drummond, I achieved an uneasy stability, keeping the spasms, which would not entirely go away, from reaching a level of intensity that would stop my forward progress. I finally settled on running hard until it felt like a spasm was about to start, transitioning to 20 steps of fast walking, and then repeating the sequence.

Drummond was at about the half-way point of the race, and I passed it with about 15 minutes to spare. In theory, crossing the half-way point of a race like this should provide a boost of confidence. But I had learned that I needed to think more in terms of Alveston, a few kilometers further and the highest point remaining on the course, as the real half-way point. After Alveston, there would still be countless inclines, including three of the five big hills (Bothas Hill,

Fields, and Cowies), but the downhill segments strongly predominated. I just need to get to Alveston, I kept telling myself; it will all be downhill from there.

Shortly after Drummond, we came upon Arthur's Seat. This was a notch in a rock face on the side of the road where Arthur Newton, who won the race five times in the 1920s, would sit for a few minutes and smoke a pipe before completing the second half of the race. There is a Comrades legend that runners who pay tribute to Arthur by going up to the notch and greeting the former champion with a "Morning, Arthur" will be rewarded with a strong second half of the race. In thinking about the race, I had expected to move past the rock without stopping. Now, feeling the distance I had already covered—more than a marathon—and with my body in rebellion, I felt compelled to join the line of runners paying their respects. I touched the rock, gave Arthur the traditional greeting, and continued on. I finally reached Alveston, pleased to have gotten there, but the mental struggle persisted. There was one internal voice that was convinced there was no way I could finish the race and another that argued, strongly, that I could. Neither one could silence the other. But there was a third, consistent voice, and I was determined to listen to it all costs. Whatever happened, I told myself, I would not quit. I would either finish or get cut.

Making the mental decision not to quit is especially important in Comrades, where the means for doing so are uniquely convenient. The bailer buses don't just sit and wait at the cut-offs. They also roam the course, and the folks who operate them are notorious for trying to coax slow, in-distress, runners into quitting and climbing on the bus. Anyone who took the bait and climbed on board immediately had a line drawn through their bib so that they couldn't change their mind and jump back on the course, which many wanted to do upon realizing the enormity of what they had just done. I was determined not to let that happen to me.

After Alveston, the main downhill portion of the down run began. It really was long and for the most part consistent. When the uphills came, they were generally short, and I just tried to do whatever everyone around me was doing, which was typically walking. I was still able to keep the leg issues from stopping me completely and was on track to make the fourth cut-off, but I was now a few minutes behind my 11:50 schedule.

I tried to distract myself by paying greater attention to the countryside, reminding myself that I was running in Africa and that I should appreciate the experience. We were in the Valley of a Thousand Hills and the views were expansive and beautiful. The runners themselves were also an interesting distraction. Some had their age stitched on the back of their jersey. I was impressed to see a few who were over 70. I also looked closely at the bibs of runners as I passed them or, more often, as they passed me. At Comrades, the bib lists your number of prior finishes. Runners, like me, whose bib said 0 finishes were not the ones to follow since they had never previously conquered the course. Those with ten or more finishes had a green background on their bib, indicating that they had received a "green number," one that had been reassigned to them each time they had successfully finished the race and that was now permanently theirs. Someone with a green number obviously knew what they were doing, but there was always the chance that they were not particularly invested in this year's race. The ones that people said to follow had a bib with a yellow background, signifying 9 finishes. They were chasing a coveted green number and would do anything to get across the finish line. But taking in the scenery and ruminating about the other runners could only distract me for a few minutes here and there. The constant mental strain about my progress still dominated.

My battle with right leg spasms continued. I wondered whether I should pull over for a leg massage. I remembered what both Bruce Fordyce and Lindsay Parry had said about not bothering with the massages – Fordyce had joked that these young physical therapists don't want to be touching your old, sweaty legs. But eventually I concluded that I had nothing to lose and pulled over to get one. Moving with lightning speed, a PT rubbed Arnica gel on my hamstrings and calves. It did seem to help and within less than a minute I was moving again. After deciding that the first one had been worth it, over the next few hours I did it two more times, each time feeling like there had been some benefit.

I made the fourth cut off but was still behind the schedule on my laminated card. I knew by this point that I had completed the longest of the seven little runs, and that was reassuring. And then, distracted by my various struggles, I tripped over a reflector in the middle of the road – what the South Africans call cat eyes. These extend straight up for about an inch and race reports regularly warned about them – but over the hours of running and with all my concerns over spasms, nutrition and the cut-offs, I had completely forgotten. I hit the cat eye and tripped, feeling myself falling forward. Instinctively I sped up and fought to stay upright, somehow pulling out of the dive. It seemed like a miracle that I hadn't fallen.

With a few kilometers to go, I was confident that I would make Pinetown, the fifth cut-off, and did so with four minutes to spare. A common Comrades expression is that the race starts at Pinetown, with slightly less than 20 km left. Certainly, by that point I knew the outcome was very much in doubt but, on the other hand, was glad to have made it as far as I had and to still be functioning. I still felt like my walking was about as fast as it had been at the beginning and my running, for the periods of time that I could do it, also seemed strong.

The final cut-off before the stadium was at Sherwood, 11 kilometers ahead. I started to do the math, going back and forth about my chances to finish. The consequences of my slowing pace were becoming more apparent with the tighter margins I was experiencing at the cut-offs. In theory, I could still get there, but I would have to pick it up, and it was hard to imagine that I could generate peak performance at this stage. I realized that if I barely made Sherwood, I would only have an hour to cover the last 9 km (about 5.6 miles), which was clearly going to be impossible at the speed I was going.

As I was getting closer to Sherwood, I calculated that I had a 4-5-minute cushion to clear the cut-off. I was starting to think that if I could keep up my current pace, the addition of those precious minutes might give me a chance at finishing. But I had not counted on one last significant hill, which I later found out was called 45th Cutting. It was longer than I had expected, and I really had nothing in me to run it. As I climbed, I realized my cushion was slowly slipping away. I kept hoping that I would reach the top and be able to run again, but the hill seemed to go on forever. Runners are alerted to the cut-offs with signs indicating when they are one kilometer out. When I saw the one-kilometer warning for Sherwood, I already knew I wouldn't make it. A shout from a bystander a short while later, with the cut-off less than a quarter of a mile away, that I still had two minutes caused me to pick up the pace. Perhaps with the exhaustion of the day I had become confused about timing, or maybe the cut-off had been mismeasured. All of that was wishful thinking. With less than a hundred yards to go, people started to tell me to slow down, that I had missed it. I eased off and jogged to the cut-off, a line of bailer buses pulling up on my right. My Comrades adventure was over.

CHAPTER 18

Craziest Fucking Thing

A bunch of us racers, all beaten by the same cut-off, milled around, waiting to board the buses. Some were in good spirits, getting photographed in front of the Sherwood cut-off sign. Others were clearly upset to have been cut, their dream of ending the day with a Comrades medal shattered. As I had crossed the timing mats marking the cut-off, I stopped my Garmin. I studied it as I got ready to board. I had missed the cut-off by less than 2 minutes. But I was more focused on the other data as I looked at the display. I had completed 81 km and run for slightly more than 11 hours. The 81 km translated into 51 miles, which gave me a good feeling. I had run farther than a 50-miler. My average pace was 12:56 minutes-per-mile, four seconds slower than the 12:52 average that in theory would have allowed me to cover the distance within the time limit.

I was philosophical as I waited to board. I was proud that I had kept my promise to myself to run until I either succeeded or was cut. I had also made it past all five of the big hills, had reached the outskirts of Durban, and had finally seen a single-digit kilometer marker. Had I barely made the cut-off instead of just missing it, there was no way I would have been able to cover the last nine kilometers in 60 minutes and cross the finish line before the 12-hour mark. In my dilapidated state, making the cut-off would have meant 75-90 minutes of torture on the road to the stadium, with the certainty that I would be arriving too late to officially finish. After we boarded the bus, all of us having enormous difficulty climbing up the stairs, we drove to the stadium along the remainder of the race route. I saw runners with no chance dragging themselves along: one guy completely sprawled out, motionless, on the side of the road and another getting loaded onto a stretcher. Those sights certainly reinforced the internal voice that was arguing that the race had done me a favor by cutting me, sparing me more than an hour of additional, pointless agony.

I met up with Josh at the stadium. It was a beautiful setting. It would have been amazing to have entered it with time to finish. Part of what had drawn me to Comrades was a type of description I had always seen. Some version of "it's the Super Bowl, the World Series and the Boston Marathon, combined!" I thought the songs and traditions at the start were everything I had imagined, the most moving I had ever experienced in a race. But other than that, it had been a fairly solitary experience in terms of fan support. It is possible that things could have been different for those last few miles in the streets of Durban, which are so much easier for friends and family to access. The thing I was most sorry to have missed was the excitement of entering the stadium, running around the track, and crossing the finish line in front of thousands of screaming spectators.

My legs were completely stiff and racked with pain as Josh and I exited the stadium. We tried to get an Uber, but there was a lot of traffic and it took a while. The pain and exhaustion that I now felt was unlike anything I had ever experienced after a long race. At one point, I turned to Josh and said: "That was the craziest fucking thing I've ever done." I would never, I assured him, do that again. We finally got back to the hotel, and, with great difficulty, I showered and climbed into bed. I slept for the next 15 hours. Josh and I went to breakfast the next morning before he would be leaving Durban for the sightseeing part of his trip to South Africa. All around, I saw people wearing their finishers medals, walking stiffly, relishing their success from the prior day. I remained philosophical, but I couldn't help but think how nice it would have been to be one of them.

Later that day, there was a post-race party for international runners at a nearby restaurant called "California Dreaming." I was excited to go; finisher's medal or not, I wanted to soak up the Comrades vibe for just a little while longer. As I walked in, I noticed on a table a stack of the Comrades road-closure signs that I had seen everywhere the last few days. I really wanted one; it seemed like the perfect souvenir. I went up to one of the organizers and asked about them. He said I could buy one for $10 or would get one for free if I would speak later when the festivities got underway. I opted to pay. I did not want to bring down the positive mood with my tale of a near miss.

The first of the finishers to speak was Ann Ashworth, the female champion. I was amazed that she was there and really taken with her. She was a local runner who was down-to-earth and obviously euphoric to have won the race. She told of running past Lindsey Parry, who was standing on the side of the road, just outside the stadium. As she went by, he looked at her and deadpanned, drawing out each word: "Nice ... fucking ... job." She was followed by a succession of ordinary finishers. For each, completing the race was the culmination of a long odyssey. I have always been a sucker for these kinds of stories. Bruce Fordyce was there and again spoke—as funny, inspiring and good-natured as he had been at the Thursday event. When the speeches were over, I went up to him with my road sign and got his autograph. That keepsake provided some solace for the disappointment at not having finished.

I had been able to get to the party but was still not myself physically. I was moving slowly and feeling depleted, and when it was over I headed back to the hotel and went straight to bed for another 15 hours. The next day, Tuesday, I had a flight out in the afternoon. Thirty hours of sleep across two days had still not been enough to restore me. I had pain in my legs and a general feeling of weakness. It was like having the flu but without the headache or fever. In some ways, it made me feel good to be in such bad shape. It reassured me that I really had left it all out there, that I had given it my best shot.

It was a struggle to get to the airport. After clearing security and making it to my gate, I found three open seats to lay across, The very idea of sitting upright seeming like more effort than I was capable of. I had at least anticipated my condition and purchased a business class ticket for the flight from Johannesburg to London. Immediately after takeoff, I put my seat into a fully horizontal position to rest some more. During the night, I needed to go to the bathroom. I got up, made it inside, and locked the door. After peeing, my knees buckled, and I dropped to the floor. Panic seized me. If a flight attendant were to find me, I thought, I would get sent to a hospital in London and prevented me from continuing to my next flight, back to New York. I broke into a sweat as I tried to rally. Finally, after a couple of minutes, I was able to pull myself up and stagger back to my seat. I lay back down, my entire upper body covered in a cold sweat, as though a fever had just broken. I stayed in that position until the flight was nearly over. With that rest—and a bottle of water and breakfast—I felt a lot better by the time we got to London and was able to finish the trip back without any further mishap.

CHAPTER 19

Atlantic City

A few months before Comrades, I had decided to go for a half-Ironman/70.3 the following summer and then, a year after that, a full one. In the weeks after returning to New York, I reconsidered that timetable. I wanted to do something to remove any lingering bad taste from having not finished, and the thought of waiting an entire year for that to happen just seemed too much. It also didn't seem necessary. Once the post-race pain and weakness had finally subsided, I could feel that I still had a ton of residual fitness from all the Comrades training. I went on the Ironman website and saw that there was a half-Ironman in Atlantic City in September, still a few months away. Having just run for 11 hours, I reasoned that a six-plus-hour half-Ironman had to be within reach with just a little more training, primarily focused on the bike. I decided to advance everything by 12 months. I would go for 70.3 in September and then, in the summer of 2019, take on the full Ironman.

I signed up for Atlantic City and tried to figure out my training. After a few days of poking around in several

Ironman Facebook groups, I found my solution. Everyone seemed to be recommending a couple of Ironman training books by Don and Melanie Fink, one for the 70.3 and one for a full Ironman. The Fink books were exactly what I needed—readable, informative, and practical. They also included common-sense training plans for three different levels of athlete: "Just Finish," "Intermediate" and "Competitive." I decided to go with the Just Finish plan and framed out my training for the following 12 weeks until race day. I dusted off my tri bike, which I hadn't used in a few years, and started doing long rides in Central Park, where each loop around the park was about six miles. It felt great to again be focused on a new goal, and the decision to accelerate my quest for an Ironman felt exactly right.

I was nervous and excited as I got in line for packet picket-up the day before the race. The Atlantic City 70.3 was an official "Ironman" race, and the dot-M Ironman logo was everywhere. That logo had its own special mystique, and getting a dot-M tattoo was a rite of passage for many finishers of their first full 140.6. Ironman, like Comrades, has its own passionate, secret society of fanatics. I liked that.

Race morning found me standing in the swim corral, anxious about what lay ahead. I knew I had eight and a half hours to finish and was sure I could do it, even if it was ugly. Still, it was intimidating to be standing at the start of something I had never accomplished before. Also, having just gotten my first Did Not Finish (DNF), I was afraid that this could be the start of a new trend and desperately wanted to avoid a second failure in a row. I was quiet, not talking to the other racers except to ask someone for help zipping up my wetsuit. A group of guys near me were chatting. As we all got ready to start, one of them fist-bumped the others and then fist-bumped me as well, a welcome gesture that helped loosen me up.

The swim was in a protected channel, and my sighting was much better than it had ever been, my tendency to pull to the left still there but not as pronounced as in prior open-water swims. Although the swim went well, it was the only part of the entire day, thrashing in the black water under a dark morning sky, where some negative thoughts slipped in. But they didn't linger, and eventually I found my rhythm and never felt any sense of fatigue as I completed the single-loop course. It felt great to be on the bike, a successful swim behind me. With the weather mild and the course flat, I was moving well. Early on, I tried to keep an eye on my speed, to keep it between 15 and 16 mph, but found myself pulling up into the high teens and sometimes over 20 mph. I decided not to worry about it as long as it felt like the pedaling was effortless, as though the bike was doing the work and not my legs.

It started raining early during the bike leg and kept up for the entire rest of the race. The rain only seemed to be a danger when making sharp turns, and all of us slowed down a great deal for those. The biggest issue with the bike was that it was 2 ½ loops and it seemed like there were always fast riders coming up from behind at high speed and not always calling out that they were passing. On my second loop, I saw a slow rider ahead on the right, somebody passing her on her left, and then a very fast rider passing on the extreme left without any warning. The rider in the middle moved farther to the left and the guy on the outside called out, "woah, woah, woah!" The two collided, went down, and slid. Watching it all sent a jolt of nervous energy through me. At another point, I saw two riders on the side of the road, one of them with blood on his face. Soon after that, I saw a woman wearing a cervical collar being loaded into an ambulance. Clearly, the bike leg was where the danger was.

It wasn't until mile 53 that I felt my legs getting a bit tired. When I got off the bike, however, I felt surprisingly good as I walked through transition. I racked my bike, dropped my helmet, and changed shoes. I then walked briskly to the exit and started running. In past triathlons I had felt a letdown going from the speed of the bike to the relative slowness of a run pace. This time I was so glad to have safely finished the bike that I did not feel any letdown at all.

I had some slight left knee pain early in the run, but it went away quickly. To my surprise, the run never really hurt. It was a little hard at the beginning, just in terms of realizing how much I still had left to run as I passed the markers for miles 1, 2 and 3. As I got to the marker for mile 4, I told myself that I had finished nearly one-third of the run and at mile 6, that I was close to half-way. The last couple of miles went by quickly. For the finish, in true Ironman corporation style, we ran along a carpeted path decorated with the dot-M logo, which was exhilarating. All in all, it was a remarkable race. I never had one come together quite so nicely, finishing each of the three legs (swim in under 44 minutes, bike in 3 hours 7 minutes, and run in 2 hours 26 minutes) faster than I had expected. With that finish, the first part of my post-Comrades plan was behind me. Now it was on to the full Ironman.

CHAPTER 20

Bear Mountain

After Atlantic City, my priority was to select a specific Ironman for the next summer. I had to choose fairly quickly both because these races often sell out and because I wanted to be able to focus my long-term training toward a particular calendar date. I looked for a race that had a friendly course but also, based on something I read on Facebook, one occurring at a time of year that would allow me to bike outside during the months of training leading up to race day. For someone then living in New York, that was a limiter. It meant picking a summer race rather than a fall one. I settled on Mont Tremblant in Quebec, Canada, which was scheduled for August.

I signed up and started to get serious about my training, now following the full-Ironman Just Finish plan from the Finks. As I looked toward the race, the thing that most concerned me was my lack of distance biking experience. My longest ride ever had been the 56-mile bike leg in Atlantic City. A good performance on the bike was critical to Ironman success for two reasons. The bike leg was the longest portion of the race, which meant that a good bike performance had the greatest potential to impact finishing time of any of the three race legs. The second reason was that the stronger you were on the bike, the less depleted you would be for the run, which was the second longest race leg. Unfortunately for me, the most important part of the race was also the one in which I had the least experience and proficiency.

The distance standard for serious cyclists is a 100-mile ride—a century—the biking equivalent of the marathon for runners. I did some research and found that, fortuitously, there would be a century in New York in May, timed almost perfectly before Mont Tremblant. I signed up and looked forward to knocking it off and removing a critical piece of doubt about my ability to successfully complete a full Ironman. The race—Gran Fondo New York (GFNY)—was scheduled to start on the George Washington Bridge over the Hudson River. The course then headed upstate over a series of hills toward Bear Mountain, 50 miles away. Riders who had signed up for a 50-miler would finish there and board buses for a ride back to the city. Those doing the full century would turn around and ride the 50 miles back to the start. I didn't give the course very much thought. I barely studied the topography, assuming that my rides in Central Park, each loop of which included a fairly steep climb called Harlem Hill, was sufficient preparation for anything the course might throw at me.

My first inkling that I might be in over my head came on a subway platform on my way to the race start. I struck up a conversation with another racer and asked if he had done GFNY before. He had. It was great he said but warned me that the course was really hilly. I had mounted onto my bike frame a course profile sticker that I received at packet pick-up and now, for the first time, really looked at it closely. I could see from the sharply jutting peaks what he was referring to, though I had no sense how difficult those might be.

It was windy and cold on the George Washington Bridge as we waited for the race to get underway. After the start, we exited the bridge into New Jersey and rode steadily uphill through a park along the Hudson. It was slow going and not just for me. At one point I noticed another rider, off to my left, slow almost to a stop and then flop over. As the hilly sections kept coming, I began to recognize that I had unwittingly chosen an especially challenging course for my first century. As the hours ticked past accompanied by a steady rise in temperature, I found the hills more and more frustrating. I was either grinding uphill at single-digit speeds, at one point going only 4 mph on a particularly steep climb, or hurtling downhill at more than 30 mph. The final climb to Bear Mountain alone extended for an exasperating 4.5 miles.

For the first 20 miles of the race, I was on track to turn in a respectable time in the 6-hour range, but as the hills multiplied, I realized it was going to be a much longer day than that. By the end, I was just determined to break nine hours and salvage the smallest amount of pride from the effort, while acutely aware that it would translate into an average pace that would never get me through an Ironman bike leg in sufficient time to be allowed to continue to the run. Like Comrades, Ironman also had a set of intermediate cut-offs.

I finally reached the top of Bear Mountain, fried from the long climb. I saw signs pointing toward the finish line for those who were doing the 50-mile race. I thought about how nice it would feel to just end it right there. But, of course, I knew that I had to finish. The top of the mountain had a well-stocked aid station and I was at least able to reward myself with some food for having made it this far, before reluctantly climbing back onto my bike for the second part of the ride. It was a tedious process - a long, slow, painful ride back to Manhattan. Finally, after hours of climbing and descending and with a sub-9-hour finish just within sight, I found myself back in the park on the New Jersey side of the Hudson and soon after that on the final stretch to the finish.

My apartment was five miles away, a straight shot down a bike path along the river. Before the race I had imagined myself pedaling home after finishing. Exhausted, I now had no appetite for that and instead called for an Uber Black that could take me and my bike back home. As I waited for the car to arrive, my legs cramped up. Just standing by the side of the road was agony. Finally, the car arrived, and I loaded my bike in the back and settled in for the short ride to my apartment. As we drove, all I could think about was how spent I was, even though the ride was 12 miles shorter than an Ironman bike leg, and how there was no way I could take on a marathon in that state. I couldn't even stay awake for the whole drive, dozing on and off until we were outside of my apartment building.

CHAPTER 21

Regrouping

A few months before GFNY, I had learned that Don Fink did private coaching, and I had signed up. Though his Ironman book was excellent, I felt that working with a live coach would enable me to get a plan that was more specific to my needs. I also thought it would help keep the inevitable doubts and negative thoughts at bay. My training had seemed to be on track before GFNY, but I was really disturbed by my performance on race day. I certainly did not feel that I was within less than three months of being ready for an Ironman. That was especially so with Mont Tremblant as my target race, which I had come to realize had a hilly bike course. Within hours of finishing GFNY, I started to completely rethink my Ironman plans. I needed more time to train and, because climbing was not my strong suit, I needed a race with a flatter bike route.

A few years earlier, I had read a book called *You Are an Ironman*, which followed six first-timers as they took on Ironman Arizona. The title of the book came from the line that the race announcer calls out to every finisher, a benediction of sorts that confirms one's ascension to the Ironman ranks. Even though it had a relatively flat bike course, I had ruled it out because it was a fall race, which meant that some of my longest training rides would take place in October and early November, when the New York weather would likely be harsh for outdoor cycling. However, with my confidence shattered by GFNY, I decided that it was a trade worth making, and Don agreed.

With the extra time on the calendar, we decided that I would do Atlantic City again in September. On race morning, after a 30-minute delay because of lightning in the area, we entered the water. The swim felt good, and my sighting seemed to have improved. But I again felt an emotional low point early on as I worked to find a rhythm in the morning darkness with the chaos of so many other swimmers thrashing around me. My mind raced to what it would feel like to take on twice the distance, but I was able to push those thoughts away and finished the swim a minute faster than the year before.

My speed on the bike was even better than it had been in 2018. I was able to trim my time by seven minutes, coming within 35 seconds of breaking three hours. I was slow right from the beginning of the run, however, and I knew right away that I would not be following up my improvements in the swim and the bike with a faster run leg than in 2018. Still, within a couple of miles I felt no residual fatigue from the bike and settled into a rhythm. All in all, it had been a good, relaxed day and just the kind of confidence-builder I needed after GFNY.

CHAPTER 22

Cold Shock

I completed my remaining workouts without incident, solving the fall weather issue by shifting my bike training to one of the spin bikes at my gym. As with Comrades, I had been surprised at how my body had reacted to the added training volume. Far from feeling broken down or exhausted from more than 12 hours per week of exercise, I was feeling strong and energetic. Most days I was doing double workouts—either a run and bike or a bike and a swim—and my body was rising to the occasion. I would find myself walking briskly to the gym at 6:00 in the morning, a bag of swim gear slung over one shoulder, a bag of my other workout gear over the other, feeling like Superman. It was unexpected and exhilarating.

The Thursday before race day I did my final swim and then flew out that afternoon to Arizona with my girlfriend Orlie. (My divorce had been finalized earlier that year.) On Friday, I headed to the race expo to check in and attend a pre-race briefing. It was amazing to realize that something that I had been thinking about for over 18 months—and that for years had thought too impossible even to consider—was about to take place.

I was staying with Craig, another one of my brothers, who lives in Arizona. We went back to his house for dinner. My oldest son Danny and oldest daughter Abby arrived from back East later that evening, full of energy and excited about being there for the big day. After spending some time with them, I tried to get to bed at a reasonable hour, hoping for a good night's sleep on that all-important "night before the night before" a big race.

The logistical demands for Ironman were a welcome distraction as my stress level climbed on Saturday. There were four bags to pack, all labeled with my race number: one for the transition to the bike, one for the transition to the run, a bike "special needs" bag that I could access on the bike course, and a run "special needs" bag that I could grab during the run. After I dropped off my bags and my bike, I walked out to take a closer look at the swim course, which was now fully adorned with its race-day buoys. It was immensely long. I knew, of course, that it would be twice as long as Atlantic City, but seeing it laid out was a different matter. I noticed that after entering the water I would swim for a short distance and then make two quick right turns before heading out on a long straightaway that would take me under a distant bridge. I would then turn left to cross the lake, make a second left to come back in the reverse direction and would need to cover an even longer straightaway that would take me under three bridges before I turned back across the lake for the finish. By the time I was done studying the layout, I was thoroughly intimidated.

As the day progressed, I found myself increasingly anxious about the race. I believed that my training had gone well, and I tried to convince myself that I was ready. While time pressure had invariably led me to do the lesser amount when Don Fink had given me a range of workout durations, I had done virtually every workout faithfully and was injury-free. On the other hand, over the past couple of weeks I had not been as euphorically high-energy as I had been a few weeks earlier, when that Superman feeling really predominated. That made for a robust internal debate over just how ready I truly was to take on the next day's challenge.

Back at Craig's house for dinner, I excused myself early from a movie that the group was watching so that I could get to bed by 10. Before turning in, I confirmed that I had organized everything I would need for race morning—bathing suit, wetsuit, googles, swim cap, booties, and my morning nutrition. Satisfied that it was all there, I set my alarm for 4:50, climbed into bed and, with less effort than expected, soon fell asleep.

I woke up at 4:10 and, unable to go back to sleep, read until it was time to get up, consciously trying to distract myself. I got out of bed at 4:50 as planned, dressed, and ate a pre-race snack. Orlie and I were on the road by 5:10, and I was at my bike by 5:45, giving me ample time to do everything I needed to do before transition closed at 6:30.

Almost immediately, I realized my first mistake of the day. All around me people were filling their bike bottles. I had put my liquids in my T1 bag, with the plan of filling the bottles after completing the swim and right before I walked the bike toward the exit. I shrugged it off, having already resolved not to concern myself over an extra couple of minutes in transition during what was certain to be a very long day. After checking to make sure my bike tires were still inflated, I put on the bottom half of my wet suit, grabbed my goggles and swim cap, and then left transition to find Orlie. Together we headed toward the swim start.

Once there, I had to make one of my first meaningful decisions of the day: where to seed myself, which would be based on my anticipated time to complete the swim. I debated between the 1:40 and the 1:50 group and decided to compromise by choosing the faster time but positioning myself near the back, just before the 1:50 swimmers. As I stood with the other racers, I drank two bottles of Gatorade, part of Don's pre-race nutrition advice. I asked Orlie to zip up my wetsuit and took off the hoodie I had been wearing. The others arrived—Craig, his daughter Maya, Danny and Abby—all in high spirits. It made for a festive atmosphere as we posed for last-minute photos. The pros were allowed to enter the water for a brief pre-race swim, and then it was time for the national anthem.

After Orlie and the others headed off, I started talking with a guy standing next to me and asked if he had done the race before. He said that he had. One thing that had been weighing on me was the design of the bike course. It called for three out and backs, each consisting of an 18.5 five mile "out" and the same distance "back." I was aware that each "out" included an uphill section and, though most race descriptions tended to minimize the steepness of the climb, I wasn't convinced that I shouldn't be worried about it. I asked about it, and the guy said it wasn't really that steep but warned me that there would also be headwinds. The flip side, he told me, was that you could really fly on the way down.

As the firing of the starting gun drew nearer, I felt my spirits lifting for the first time in days. The adrenaline was pumping, and I felt a sense of determination and excitement about the race. The big day that I had spent so much time preparing for was actually here. The gun went off, and we began to slowly move forward. Orlie called my name for a picture, and I gave a big thumbs up with both arms raised. As I approached the final stretch before the water, I heard a race official tell us to separate into five lanes. A volunteer stood at the front of each. There was a beep every few seconds and then the volunteers would turn to the side to let the next group of five enter the water. Suddenly, I was at the front and, following the beep, I moved forward into the lake, walking until it was deep enough to swim.

I transitioned into a breaststroke, keeping my head out of the water as I navigated among the crowd of swimmers past the two sharp right turns that would lead me to the long straight section toward the distant bridge. The second turn completed, it was time to switch to freestyle. For the first time, I put my head into the water. I pulled it out immediately, gasping. It was much colder than I had expected. I quickly tried to put it in again, with the same result. I swam a few more strokes with my head out before trying another time, only to again be unable to keep it in. I tried switching briefly to breaststroke, putting my head in the water between strokes at a slower pace than I would for freestyle, but I still couldn't keep my face submerged.

My heart was racing, and I could feel panic setting in. I had noticed a swimmer go to one of the kayaks shortly before I entered the water and now realized that he must have either bailed or gone there to regroup. My mind raced with thoughts of bailing and how horrible it would be to drop out now. To train for the better part of a year, fly across the country, and then, with two of my kids, my girlfriend, my brother, and my niece watching, drop out of the race after only a couple of minutes would be humiliating. And how would I explain it? "It was so cold; you had to be there to understand!" Yet, they were watching as virtually every one of the other 2,500 racers was able to continue. They would be sympathetic but, inside, would no doubt be thinking, "What the hell?"

I could not let it end this way. I had to get things under control. I told myself, out loud, to "calm down" and to "just breathe." I kept trying to put my face in the water and finally was able to keep it in without hyper-ventilating. I took a few normal strokes and suddenly realized it would all be okay. As I settled into a rhythm, I noticed that the sky was getting lighter, making me feel even more tangibly that I was coming out of the darkness of those terrifying first moments. A deep feeling of well-being came over me as I headed toward the distant bridge.

CHAPTER 23

Buoy to Buoy

During my study of the swim course from the day before, I had thought carefully about how I should be "chunking" the various parts of the race. Don Fink had written about the importance of mentally breaking down the three legs into smaller parts and limiting your focus to the current one. Done right, this would head off the depression that could come from constantly thinking about the immense amount of racing still ahead. It was like the Comrades strategy of only focusing on the distance to the next cut-off, rather than the monumental amount of running still left to the stadium.

I had thought that I would divide the swim into four segments. The first long straightaway to the distant bridge, the short swim across the lake, the longer straightaway coming back in the reverse direction, and then the final short section to the swim exit. Now that I was in the water, with the panic gone, I recognized that my plan would never work. The distances of the straightaways were simply too great to serve as a proper "chunk." The buoys, on the other hand, were spaced a few hundred yards apart. That was how I needed to think about the swim I decided, to just focus on going from "buoy to buoy." With my confidence growing, I picked off one buoy after another and, in what seemed like a surprisingly short amount of time, saw the distant bridge coming into view. I passed underneath it and then made the turn to the other side of the lake, where I would begin the journey back in the reverse direction. The short swim across the lake brought on yet another rush of good feeling.

I stayed focused on the "buoy to buoy" strategy. There were other swimmers around me and I experienced the occasional bump of light contact. But the field was far more spread out than at Atlantic City and I was not stressed. I also now realized that my seeding decision had been spot on. I was swimming a little faster than most of those around me, and passing felt a lot better than being passed.

Again, with surprising suddenness, I realized that the first of the three bridges that I would pass for the return was within sight. My confidence continued to grow as I swam under each. I passed the last bridge and saw the final turn buoy. I swam around it and headed toward the shore. My shoulders were a bit tired but, in general, the swim had been less taxing than I had feared. My excitement built as I picked out the precise exit point up ahead and swam for it. As I got closer, I saw volunteers in light blue shirts on both sides of the exit, partially in the water with hands extended. One of them grabbed my hand just as I started to stand. I climbed out of the water with the volunteer's help and moved up a ramp. I walked into a flat area where there were peelers on both sides and headed to one on the right. The peeler helped with my top and then had me sit while he got the legs off. He handed me the wet suit, and I started walking briskly toward transition. I glanced at my watch. I had completed the swim in 1:24—much better than my pre-race estimate of 1:40.

It was cool, but I barely noticed, thrilled to be out of the water, the terror of the first few moments behind me. I had completed an Iron-distance swim –twice as far as I had ever gone in a race and longer than any single training session. It was an accomplishment in its own right, regardless of whatever else might happen during the rest of the long day still ahead of me. I heard my name, looked up, and there was the group. I high-fived Danny and Abby and kept moving, now breaking into a trot at their encouragement. Orlie ran alongside me and asked if I wanted to give her the wet suit. I handed it to her and entered transition.

I was directed to the men's dressing tent. As I prepared to enter, a volunteer handed me my transition bag. I found a seat just inside. I sat down, opened my bag, and started to pull things out. There was a note that Orlie had sneaked into my bag:

Transition 1
Swim Done!
Deep breath
One step at a time . . . .
You can do this!!
Love you!!!

It put an immediate smile on my face.

I toweled off, removed my wet bathing suit, and changed into the tri shorts. I put on my tri top, socks, and shoes, applied Vaseline, and grabbed all the other supplies that I had placed into the bag the day before. I left the tent and headed toward where my bike was. I heard my number called out. To my surprise, a volunteer brought me my bike, which meant that I didn't have to go looking for it. I had started to fill my bottles when another volunteer came over and offered to do that for me. While he did that, I tried to stuff everything else from my bike bag into my shirt pockets. Amidst all this activity, two other volunteers came up and offered to apply sunscreen, which I gladly accepted. That allowed me to throw away my own sunscreen, which I now realized I had no room for. I crammed in my gels, took my bike, and headed for the exit.

Outside of transition, at the designated point, I climbed onto the bike and started pedaling. Just then, I again heard my name and looked up to see the group. I waved as I rode through the chute toward the exit. As I passed over the timing mat, I clicked my watch to mark the end of transition. It had taken me 19 minutes in total, a bit embarrassing even by my own lax standards. Still, it didn't dampen my spirits as I headed out for the second leg of the day.

The first few miles were flat as we moved through city streets, and then, within a couple of miles, we were on a desert road. The climb began a little more than ten miles into the ride, about at the time I expected it. As if on cue, a headwind also picked up and I was glad the guy at the swim start had told me to expect it. My speed almost immediately dropped. It had been as high as 19 mph on the flats but now dropped below 12 mph. I was on a divided highway and looking across, I could see riders really moving on the downhill and knew that I at least had that to look forward to.

Early in that first "out" segment I worried that I may have set the angle of the aero bars too low when I had reassembled the bike in my brother's garage, and that I would pay a price for it over the length of the ride. But I just wasn't sure, perhaps it was all in my head. I decided to leave it alone and keep riding. I made it to the top of the climb and saw that the turnaround was just a few hundred yards ahead. As I made the turn, I glanced at my watch. I had been riding for about 1:21. If I multiplied that by six it would translate into an 8-hour ride, much slower than my goal of seven hours. I decided to reserve judgment until finishing the downhill segment, which I assumed would be considerably faster. Given the success of my "buoy to buoy" strategy on the swim, I resolved to apply something similar to the bike. I decided that each "out" and each "back" would be a single "box" and that my goal would be to check each box. When I looked at the distance display on my watch, it would only be for purposes of figuring out which portion of my current box I had completed and how much I had left before I could add another check mark.

With the first box "checked," I headed downhill. My speed picked up almost immediately. At one point, I saw that I was going 27 mph, so fast that I felt the need to take my hands off the Aero bars to make sure that I maintained control. After four or five miles, the angle of the descent lessened, but there were still a few more miles of downhill before the course leveled out and I reached the turnaround. I checked my second "box" and, looking at my watch, saw that it had taken me about 1:10. I was relieved that the "back" really had been faster than the "out," with its long climb into headwinds. While heading back up for my second "out," I also realized that checking this box would actually mean completing more than half of the ride since I would have completed two out of three uphills.

Early in my second climb I concluded that the aero bars really were way too low. I had not sufficiently tightened them during reassembly, and they had moved. I would need to get them repositioned and tightened at the first available bike mechanic station, another nice feature of Ironman. When I came to one, marked by a tent a few feet to the side of the road, I rolled my bike on the dirt and asked the mechanic if he had an Allen wrench. He did. After I moved the bars to what I hoped was the right angle, he tightened all of the screws. When he was done, he suggested that I carry the bike off the dirt and back to the road because there were thorns around. I did that and then checked both tires, which felt clear. I reached the top of the "out" section for the second time and turned for the next descent, which passed without incident. As I began my third and final climb, I was starting to feel it. I kept reminding myself to keep my head in the current box and not to think ahead to the next box, to the ride as a whole, and certainly not to the marathon that still lay ahead. It was a battle. My mind kept trying to focus on what still was to come or to pose even longer-term questions, such as whether I would ever want to do something like this again.

The pack was really thinning as I began my final climb of the day. Fast riders whom I had seen earlier were clearly ahead of me for good. I stopped to take a gel and to pee. Then, I resumed climbing, but something didn't feel right. I pulled over and looked more closely at my front tire. It was flat. I must have picked up a thorn when I rolled the bike on the dirt to the bike mechanic's station. This had never happened to me before during a race, and I had trouble believing it. Within less than a minute though, I had moved past the surprise, knowing that I just needed to focus on changing the tire. I opened the pouch that I carried behind the seat and pulled out a new tube, a tire lever, an inflator, and a CO_2 cannister. I worked the old tube out easily, put in the new one, and tried to add just a little bit of air to make it easier to position everything before re-seating the tire edge and fully inflating the new tube. However, when I tightened the CO_2 cannister onto the inflator, the air immediately started pouring out. I tried another canister. In my caution, I had purchased two at the Expo. The same thing happened again. Later, I remembered that when I had packed my bike for the trip, the inflator had a partially used cartridge still attached. Instead of simply discharging the remaining air, I had twisted off the cartridge, and there had been a loud noise. At the time, I had thought nothing of it, but I must have wrecked the inflator.

I was on a long desert stretch of the course, with no aid station anywhere in sight. As my mind raced, I noticed that my old manual pump was still attached to my bike frame. I pulled it off and took a few moments to refresh my knowledge of how it worked. I then added some air to the tube, re-seated the tire, filled the tube the rest of the way, and put the wheel back on the bike. Something was wrong, however. When I spun the front wheel, it rubbed against the brake. I tried re-positioning the tire on the forks but still couldn't get it to seat properly. In desperation, I opened the front brakes since I shouldn't need to use them anyway and began to ride again. I could feel that it still wasn't right, but at least I was moving. I decided to keep riding until I found the next mechanic's station and to get help there.

After a few slow miles I reached the next aid station. I didn't see a set-up for a bike mechanic, but one of the volunteers told me that there was a guy there who was good with tires. The volunteer called the other guy over. The tire guy immediately figured out the problem. I had not properly seated the tire in one spot and the tube was bulging. I was surprised I hadn't noticed the mistake, which was probably an indication of how stressed the whole situation had made me. He partially deflated the new tube and fully seated the tire before adding more air and putting the wheel back on the bike. From the moment I first realized I had a flat until that point, I probably lost about 30 minutes. It was a lot of time to have given up for a repair that should have taken no more than ten minutes, but I consoled myself that it had essentially forced me to rest during the hardest segment of the bike course—the third and final uphill of the day. I wondered what the group was thinking. They were tracking me on an app and must have noticed a huge slowdown.

No doubt they were questioning whether I had bonked, crashed, or even dropped out.

I finally reached the turnaround at the top and began my sixth and final box for the bike. As I headed downhill, I could see that the field was really thinning out. About six miles into the downhill, I looked across to the uphill side and saw what looked to be literally the very last guy, followed closely by a van and, behind that, a truck that seemed poised to sweep him off the course for missing a cut-off. It was a depressing sight.

There were only a few mile markers on the course, one of which was for 100-miles. I had passed it twice during earlier loops and was happy to pass it now for the final time, when it actually meant something. I looked down at my watch as I rode by. I had been on the bike for less than seven hours. It had taken me nearly nine hours to cover the same distance at GFNY, which was testament to the relative flatness of this course and my superior fitness as compared to May. Of course, I still had 12 miles to go. Those last miles were the hardest of the ride. I couldn't stay in the Aero position for more than a few minutes at a time and kept having to come back up. I continued pedaling, relieved to complete each passing mile on a course that was much quieter now, with the shadows lengthening as the sun was starting to dip. My spirits lifted as soon as I entered the chute that marked the final approach to transition. The group was there to greet me, and I called out as I passed to tell them about the flat tire.

Completing the bike leg, like coming out of the water after the swim, gave me a jolt of good feeling. As with the swim, I had done something I had never done before. In this case, I had ridden 12 miles longer than the century and far longer than any of my training rides. No matter what happened on the run, I knew I had completed an Iron-distance swim and an Iron-distance bike, and these were, for me, monumental accomplishments.

As compared to the transition from the swim to the bike, this one was straightforward. After handing my bike to a volunteer, I walked quickly to the tent, got my bag, changed into my running shoes and put on my hydration belt and hat. A clearly upbeat guy sitting across from me looked at me, said, "let's go run!" and gave me a high five before heading out. My running shoes contained a second note from Orlie, which added to my increasingly positive mood:

Wow!

Swim Done, Bike Done

Deep Breath

One step at a time . . .

You CAN DO THIS!!!

Love You!!

I moved out of the tent toward the exit, pleased to see that my legs were still functioning after seven and a half hours on the bike. Sticking with my box-checking strategy, I decided to split the run into four boxes. I had thought that the marathon course was 6.5 miles out, 6.5 miles back, 6.5 miles out, and a final 6.5 miles to the finish. Each of these, I decided, would be a single "box" that I needed to check.

At all times during the run, I would try to stay focused only on the current box.

As I took my first running steps out of transition, my legs felt surprisingly good. Not all was well, though. I felt depleted, had a cramp on my right side, and had six miles of running ahead of me before I would reach the first aid station with salt. I started with my pre-race plan of a 4-minute/1-minute run-walk ratio. Even though I had promised myself to keep focused on the current box, I needed to do some longer-term planning to figure out the run pace that I needed to maintain to finish by the 17-hour cut-off. In adding the times for my swim, bike legs, and the transitions, I realized that I could average 15-minute miles and make it with plenty of room to spare.

Still, having read lots of race reports by folks who had bonked during the run and been forced to walk the last five or even ten miles, I wanted to make sure that I targeted a pace that I could maintain all the way through to the end. I realized quickly that a 4/1 run-walk ratio was too ambitious. I progressively increased the length of the walk segments until, eventually, they were three minutes long. I was also walking the few slight uphills on the course and through the aid stations. The runners around me were in good spirits, despite the fact that we were all deep into a very long and challenging day. I had the impression that they had all done some version of the same math. They knew, like I did, that we still had lots of cushion. As long as we could just keep moving, we would be fine, we would get our medals, and we would hear those iconic words, "You are an Ironman!"

Early in the first box, I started to get nervous about the weather. The sun was fading and the temperature was dropping with surprising speed. Even though I had purchased a long-sleeve shirt specifically as a throw-away for the run, I had decided at the last minute not to put it into either my run transition or run special needs bags. I just couldn't believe it would get cold enough to need it. By the end of my first "box," the sun had fully disappeared, and the course was dark. I had never done my training runs at night and this was a new, captivating experience. The lights of the buildings along the river and from the moon provided just enough illumination to allow me to make out the contours of the nearby mountains, which made for an alluring, peaceful scene. I couldn't fully enjoy it, though. With the sun gone, the temperature kept dropping, and the cold was really starting to bother me. I couldn't fathom what had led me to not have at least put the long-sleeve shirt in my run special needs bag, which I could have picked up just a few miles into my first box. My main hope now was that Orlie would be on the run course at the halfway mark and that she would have the hoodie I had been wearing before the start of the swim. I wasn't sure what I would do if that didn't happen.

I finally got my salt at about mile 6, though by then the cramp had already resolved itself, perhaps because of the pretzels I had been grabbing at the aid stations. The cold continued to be my big challenge. It was all I could think about. After about 6.5 miles of running, I mentally checked the first box, but the turnaround was nowhere in sight. The course continued. I passed seven miles and then eight before finally reaching the turn. I had clearly misunderstood the layout. I was certain it was still two "out and backs" but wasn't sure how the math all worked to have us end at the right place with the correct mileage. As I continued through my second box, I was still running fine—albeit with longer walk breaks—with no significant pain or hamstring tightness.

Just before reaching mile 12, I found Orlie standing by the side of the road. I asked if she had the hoodie, and she said with a smile that she did and pulled it out of her backpack. I was relieved to put it on. She trotted alongside for a few minutes, upbeat and excited. She asked if I was going to be able to finish. I told her I wasn't letting myself think that far ahead but that, yes, for sure I would finish. After mile 12 we came to a split. The right led to the finish and the left to a second loop. Orlie peeled off and I headed to the left. I reached mile marker 13 a short while later, my second box checked. At around mile 15 I reached a turnaround that took me back out. It gave me a mental lift to know that I would be doing the run loop for the last time.

I felt some slowing as I pushed through my third box. My legs still felt good, but I had some pain in my arms, especially my left, and a slight headache. For a moment, a wild thought entered my head that I might be having a heart attack, but my heart rate seemed fine. I registered it as paranoia and kept on moving. Finally, after more than five hours of running, I reached mile marker 19 and the beginning of my fourth and final run box. Much earlier in the run, I had promised myself that I could start to think about finishing once I got to box 4. Now that I was there, it still seemed too rash, and I decided to stay focused only on the next few miles. At the pace I was going, I still had nearly an hour and a half left on the course. I recalibrated and decided to permit myself thoughts of crossing the finish at the mile 24 marker. As I continued my steady progress through the last quarter of the run, I saw other runners heading out in the other direction, miles behind me. I did not envy them their situation. They still had a couple of hours of slow running ahead of them and might not make it across in time.

At around mile 24, my Garmin conked out and I switched to my late-stage Comrades strategy of run/walk based on feel. I would run for a distance that felt doable, sometimes using a landmark like a light post as a target, switch to a brisk walk when it felt right to do that, and then do it over again. I was still making good progress, probably even slightly faster than when I was trying to do a more structured run/walk based on the Garmin alerts. Nevertheless, I decided that mile 24 was still too early to think about the finish, and I resolved to keep my focus only on this box.

For much of the last two miles I kept pace with another racer, and we chatted about the swim. He told me that he had also panicked and in fact had decided to bail. He had signaled to one of the kayakers by passing his hand across his throat that he was done. The kayaker had misinterpreted the hand gesture and thought he was being told to back off and did. In the next few moments, my running companion had regained his composure and, remarkably, was now poised to finish.

We passed mile marker 25 and, after what seemed like a fairly long time, I started to wonder how far we were from the finish. With my watch dead, I had no idea. I asked the other racer, and he told me that we still had .7 miles to go. Three or four minutes later, after my companion stepped off to go into a porta potty, a guy rode passed on a bike and called out that there was less than a mile to go, which left me with the impression that we still had close to a mile to run. That was depressing. A short while later, I passed a volunteer who said there were .2 miles left. That was far more like it. I was really getting close.

CHAPTER 24

You Are an Ironman

I could now make out the race announcer's voice in the distance, calling out finishers with the iconic "You are an Ironman." It was Mike Reilly, the legendary "Voice of Ironman," a fixture at finishes since 1989. My excitement built as I allowed myself, for the first time in the day, to really imagine crossing the finish line. I thought about removing my hoodie before entering the chute, to make for a better finisher's picture, but I couldn't bear the idea. It really *was* cold. I could see frost on the portion of my tri shirt above the zipper of my hoodie.

With just a few hundred yards to go, I heard my name. It was the whole group—everyone but Orlie, who was waiting at the finish to take pictures. They were excited and started to run with me. We trotted along and then, just before the chute, they veered off. The chute was surprisingly short, and suddenly the moment was upon me. I passed under the arch, marking the official finish, and raised my arms in triumph for the finisher's photo. Then, I heard

Mike Reilly say the words that I had fantasized about for months: "Jeffrey Weiss, you are an Ironman!"

I moved into a post-finish area. A volunteer grasped my right arm and moved me to another volunteer, who put on my medal, handed me a finisher's hat and shirt, gave me a solar blanket, removed my timing chip from my ankle, and then allowed me to exit to the side so that I could rejoin the group. There were hugs all around. It was wonderful to be able to share it all and great to talk about the race in the past tense, especially the swim and flat tire fiascos, both of which were already morphing into nothing more than amusing anecdotes.

My joy at finishing was further enhanced when Orlie handed me a poster that she had secretly created for the race. It was professionally done: a picture of Mike Reilly announcing finishers with the bubble, "Jeffrey Weiss, you are an Ironman!" She told me that one of the race officials had seen her holding it up at the finish and walked over, telling her that Reilly would get a kick out of seeing it and offering to take her over to meet him. Orlie showed the poster to Reilly, who autographed it. It was in my hands now, something that I knew in an instant would always be a treasured memento of the big day.

I checked the Ironman app to confirm my race time. My final time was 15:44:51. Before the race, I had hoped to finish in under 15:30, but the flat tire had put that out of reach. Still, I was glad that my final time had a 15 rather than a 16 in front of it.

I stiffened up during the car ride back to Craig's, and getting into the house was challenging. When I got to the bedroom, I started to shiver convulsively. Orlie covered me with blankets and told me to take deep breaths, and the shivering stopped. I rallied myself for a painful shower and then got back into bed, happy to be able to plan on sleeping for as long as I wanted. Before nodding off, I tried to sort out my emotions from the day. It was tremendously satisfying to have set what had been, for me, such an audacious goal and to have achieved it. I thought about how, in many ways, that finish had been nine years in the making, since that very first 10K in November of 2010, which had represented the entirety of my endurance ambitions at that time. There had been years of incremental gains since then, and only until the last year had Ironman even seemed to be within reach.

I also thought about how my fitness journey had overlapped with a dramatic reinvention in my professional life. In the same decade in which I had progressed from the 10K to Ironman, I had left the safe confines of my law practice to join a start-up as its general counsel, endured dramatic rises and falls in its fortunes (including its achievement of unicorn[1] status, followed by a bankruptcy and then a reemergence and rise to even greater heights), and acted as interim president to hold things together during its most tumultuous period. When I realized that I could be more effective with a stronger science education, I had completed a master's in biotechnology by utilizing the nine hours I was spending on airplanes each week between Maryland and Arizona. I did not regard the overlap as coincidental. There were times when I felt that something difficult that I had

---

1. A "unicorn" is the term for a privately held start-up company with a valuation in excess of $1 billion.

achieved in my fitness life gave me increased confidence to take on a new challenge professionally, and sometimes the inspiration went in the other direction. All in all, it had been a remarkably exciting and transformational decade.

With all that build-up, I wondered why I hadn't experienced a burst of euphoria right as I finished. Others certainly did, falling to their knees or breaking into tears, clearly overwhelmed at what they had just accomplished. Yet, though I didn't realize it at the time, that long day in Arizona gave me something very different and far more lasting. There has not been a single week since I crossed the finish line that I have not thought about some aspect of that race. It has generated a constant, low-level source of good feeling, a sense that, as the Ironman motto famously recites, "Anything is possible." But balanced against it has always been the memory of those first moments of terror on the swim and the realization that it all could have gone in a different, humiliating direction. With audacious goals comes the potential for great failure.

I asked myself whether I would ever do another one. My reaction, with the intensity of the day's effort still fresh in my mind, was a hard no. Certainly, I didn't come away from the race feeling that I couldn't wait to sign up for another one, which I gather is a reaction for some. And, logistically, it had been an immense challenge to fit in 10-13 hours a week of working out in an otherwise demanding life. I had adapted by getting up every morning at 5 a.m. so that I could fit in my training before the workday started, but that left me worn out by 9 p.m. and in bed, exhausted, by 10. If I did decide to do another, I told myself, it wouldn't be for the race-day experience with all its emotional intensity. Instead, it would be to recapture that Superman feeling in the last months before the race—to always have energy, to be able to come off the bike after five hours of riding, to then begin a run with energy and not a hint of discomfort, and to feel pumped rather than exhausted after the whole workout was over. If I were to do another, I concluded, it would be to once again live in the body of an Ironman.

CHAPTER 25

Return to Africa?

Immediately after Comrades, I was certain I would never try the race again. But as the months passed and the agony of that day and its immediate aftermath receded in my memory, I started to wonder. What if I tweaked my training? What if I adjusted my race-day nutrition? What about all my new experience in longer races? Sometimes, you don't achieve your dreams on the first try, I reminded myself. Should that necessarily mean that you abandon the dream? Perhaps that would be my Comrades story—ne of triumph after failure.

Nearly all participants in Comrades choose to qualify with a sufficiently fast marathon. When I had tried Comrades in 2018, the qualifying standard was five hours. The following year, they lowered it to 4:50. I had broken 4:50 five years earlier in my second Marine Corps marathon, but wasn't certain about my ability to do it again. There was another way to qualify, however. It was by completing an Ironman, regardless of the duration of your marathon split.

That long day in Arizona, I had been fighting not just to finish the race but also to qualify for Comrades, which had made it all the more challenging to stay focused on the immediate buoy or box. Qualifying with an Ironman appealed to me not just because it got me out of the need to run a fast marathon. I also liked the idea of experiencing a race that was far longer in duration than Comrades, which I reasoned would be effective in pushing out some of the negative thoughts and doubts I had faced in 2018 when I couldn't imagine racing for 12 hours.

With Ironman completed, I signed up for Comrades and, with Don Frink's help, pivoted my training back toward ultra-running. Don wanted to see me work on my speed, and we targeted a local half marathon at the end of January called the "Icebreaker," to be followed by the Los Angeles Marathon in early March.

The Icebreaker course was a loop of slightly more than 3.33 miles, which I would have to complete four times. Don wanted me to target a sub-2:15:00 finish. I wasn't sure that was possible—it would mean averaging 33:45 per lap—but resolved to give it a shot. I made my way through the first loop, surprising myself by hitting the pace required to finish in under 2:15. I held on for the next two loops and then, with no need to hold back, pushed a little harder on the last one. As I crossed the finish line, I stopped my Garmin and looked down: 2:14:02. The official race time recorded it as 2:14:00, only one second away from achieving a time that began with 2:13. Still, I had hit Don's target and gotten a new PR.

With the half-marathon behind me, the next goal was the LA Marathon in March. There as well, Don wanted to see me achieve a new personal best. I liked the idea of trying. Even though IMAZ had qualified me for Comrades, I still wanted to run a sub-4:50 for the additional confidence I thought it would give me. It was one thing to know that I could stay out on a course for more than 12 hours – it was another to be confident that I could maintain a decent speed over a long race. Given how much of the Comrades challenge was mental, I wanted to do everything in my power to remove unnecessary doubts come race day.

CHAPTER 26

I Love LA

My training for Los Angeles proceeded like clockwork. For most of January, my excitement about the upcoming race grew. I had lived in LA for four years at the beginning of my legal career some 30 years earlier and was looking forward to running a marathon in another city that had special meaning for me. I also liked the layout of the course—a point-to-point route (no herd of faster runners streaming by in the other direction) that went from Dodger Stadium to Santa Monica with its inviting views of the Pacific Ocean.

As January drew to a close and February began, I had a new worry that had nothing to do with the typical runner complaints about injuries and demanding workouts. In January, I first started to hear about the "Coronavirus," which had struck residents of a Chinese city called Wuhan. Having recalled prior virus scares—SARS, bird flu and Zika—that had never disrupted life in the U. S. and impressed by what seemed to be a determined and overwhelming government reaction in Wuhan, I was not worried about the new virus. Indeed, when a young co-worker expressed his concerns, I teased him that he had a better chance of catching bubonic plague, with all the rats running around the streets of New York, than he did of catching the Coronavirus.

But with each passing week, the news grew more troubling. The virus spread out of Wuhan, then out of China, and reached the U. S. during the third week of January. International air travel restrictions were put in place in early February and on the third of that month, the federal government declared a public health emergency. Soon, races were getting canceled. The first high profile cancelation took place on February 17 when the Tokyo Marathon organizers announced that they were eliminating mass participation for their race, scheduled for March 1. Instead, they would hold a much smaller event with just the elite runners. With each passing week more races were getting called off, yet I still held out hope for Los Angeles and, beyond that, for Comrades, which was scheduled for June. Like a lot of other runners, my early Coronavirus worries were narrowly focused on the possible impact of the virus on my racing schedule.

Los Angeles was scheduled for March 8. As February ended, the organizers were still holding firm that the race would go forward. I made my hotel and plane reservations, continued with my training, and held my breath. I got especially nervous on March 4, when county officials in Los Angeles declared a Covid-19 emergency, but the race had still not been canceled. I flew out on March 6 and checked into a hotel on the beach in Santa Monica, located just a few hundred yards from the finish line. As I was checking in, I noticed a flyer about tickets for an upcoming Los Angeles Clippers NBA game. If they are going to cancel the race, I told myself, they would also have to cancel NBA games, and there is no way they are going to do that.

This was to be the 35th running of the LA Marathon and one of the race morning announcers said that there were 131 legacy runners participating that day (folks who had run each of the 34 prior races). That was impressive. As I get older, I always like hearing stories about longevity in fitness, which give me hope that I still have a lot of time left for races. At 6:55 a. m., right on schedule, the race started, and the elite men were off. As I reached the start a few minutes later, I was delighted to hear Randy Newman's *I Love LA* blaring out, the city's unofficial anthem.

There was a short uphill out of the stadium, and then the course turned toward downtown. Once in the city there were landmarks that I remembered from years earlier, including the Superior Court building that I had gone to so many times for hearings and the Music Center across the street where I would always park. There were also the famous sites, including the police headquarters at Parker Center, familiar to anyone who watched the television show Dragnet, and the Disney Concert Hall. After a few miles, we were out of the city and running past the scenic LA neighborhood of Echo Park, on our way to Sunset Boulevard. I was taking it all in, delighting in the familiar landmarks and street names, happy about the early morning temperatures which were still in the 50s, and pleased that the course was as flat as promised. I spent a lot of time in those early miles trying to get myself dialed in with pace, looking to avoid a too-fast start and hoping for a more even effort that would get me across the finish in under 4:45, or at the very least in under 4:50.

It got very touristy after Sunset Blvd as we ran down Hollywood Blvd past the Hollywood Walk of Fame, the Chinese Theater, the intersection of Hollywood and Vine, and the Capital Records building. We even got a glimpse of the Hollywood sign off in the hills to the right. Soon, I was in West Los Angeles, where I had lived some 30 years earlier. Another stop on my personal memory tour followed as we ran past Century City and the building where I had once worked.

I had remembered from the elevation map that the last few miles were a fairly steep downhill, and I kept waiting for the start of that. As we got into the last third of the race I continued to feel pretty good: no serious hamstring tightness, toes typically sore but nothing crazy. Still, I was definitely slowing. I had been trying to keep my pace between 10:30, which would have worked out to a 4:40 finish that Don thought I was capable of, and 10:52, which translated to a 4:45 finish that I felt was more realistic. I stayed close to 10:30 for the first 10 miles, but then my pace slowly began to creep up.

Though I was still trying to figure out exactly what to think about Covid, by the time the race had started I was getting a bit nervous. This was before masks—the following week the Surgeon General would still be admonishing people to *not* wear them—but the idea of physical contact with others, at a time when everyone had become fixated on using hand sanitizer to avoid infection, seemed reckless. I avoided the classic marathon signs with a bullseye and "touch this for extra power" written on them. At several points along the route, I saw spectators holding huge, Costco-size containers of pretzels for runners to reach in and grab and that struck me as insane. Of more direct concern was one particularly joyful runner who was always nearby and who, dreadlocks flying behind him, was a one-man cheer squad, calling out encouragement and giving high fives to everyone within range. Feeling like a party-pooper, I studiously avoided eye-contact, lest I find myself on the receiving end of a high five.

The last stretch of the course took us through Santa Monica, on the way to the sea. Though my pacing had stayed within my target range, two familiar problems cropped up. The first was that I was not running the tangents, as usual, and I was getting mile alerts several tenths of a mile before the mile markers. I was kicking myself for not having looked for a pace bracelet at the Expo. The second was more serious. The temperature had stayed mild for most of the race and there had even been some stretches in Hollywood where the surrounding buildings had cast shade. But over the last few miles the spaces were more open, and the sun was higher in the sky. At about mile 25, I suddenly felt a major spasm coming on in my right hamstring. For an instant, I saw another 4:50 finish getting away, like at Steamtown. I was at about the 3-minute mark of that particular run-walk interval and quickly took action. I switched to a walk and popped the last of the salt tablets that I had picked up at the Expo. After a minute of unscheduled walking, the spasm danger seemed to have gone away, and I started running again.

With about a mile to go, we turned on to Ocean Avenue, and from about .3 miles out, I was able to see the finish line. For the first time all day, I was able to relax: a sub-4:50 finish was in the bag. I pushed hard for the last stretch, crossing at 4:47:47. I had missed a PR by about a minute but still felt like I had run a great race and was really pleased to have turned in a Comrades-qualifying time. As I moved through the finishing area, I couldn't stop thinking about how great the day had gone and what a success it had all been. First the PR at the Icebreaker and now this. It was all coming together, with Comrades 2020 just three months away.

CHAPTER 27

Best-Laid Plans

The LA Marathon would turn out to be the last big city marathon to go forward anywhere in the world in 2020. Three days later, the World Health Organization declared Covid a pandemic, and on March 13 the U. S. government declared it a national emergency. Those NBA games that I had been certain would never be canceled came to a sudden halt on March 11, three days after the LA Marathon, when the league suspended the season.

Even in the face of all that, I still held out hope that this might be short-lived. In mid-March the U. S. government was talking about "flattening the curve" within 15 days, which suggested that by the end of the month things might open up again. But the more I read about Covid, which now had my full attention, the more I could tell that things could not possibly move that fast. I continued to train as though there would be a Comrades in June, but, with each passing week, it was becoming clearer that it was not to be. On March 23, I emailed Don to tell him that I had decided to go ahead and assume that Comrades would be canceled and to start taking my training volume down. In mid-April, the Comrades race organizers bowed to the inevitable and announced that the race would not go forward.

I was still living in Manhattan and was doing most of my running in Central Park. As the wave of closures grew in those early weeks of Covid in the U. S., I became increasingly worried that I might lose my ability to run outside. Strict shelter-in-place orders were cropping up around the world in places like Hong Kong, Australia, Italy, and Israel—so restrictive that people were not allowed to be outside for any sustained period of time or to go any meaningful distance from their homes. When San Francisco adopted a similar lockdown on March 16, I worried that it was only a matter of time before other American cities would as well. None seemed a more likely candidate than New York, which was ground zero for Covid in those early weeks, experiencing more than 500 deaths a day beginning in early April, a toll that necessitated the use of freezer trucks as temporary morgues.

I did not own a treadmill and my gym had already closed, so a strict lockdown that effectively banned outdoor running would have really been a blow. With no other good fitness option, it would have been a struggle to stay fit at a time when I, like everyone else it seemed, was surrendering to all my worst eating impulses as a salve against the emotional pressures of being locked inside most of the time. To my relief, week after week, I continued to be allowed to run outside. I also pulled out my tri-bike and put it on an old trainer that I still had, allowing me to cross-train.

Then, in June, while running in Central Park I felt a twinge in my right knee. At first, I thought it was nothing. I tried several times over the next few days to run, but the pain persisted. I went to a doctor and then, with a recommendation from Don, a physical therapist, necessitating visits to deserted office buildings, my first such forays in months. I received no real diagnosis. It seemed to be a case of what is ubiquitously referred to as "runners' knee." I assumed that a few visits to the therapist would put it right, but month after month, I continued to be unable to run without pain and confined my exercise to the bike. At least, there my situation had improved. I had purchased a gym-quality spin bike a month into Covid, and the knee was not affecting my riding, which became my only exercise.

With my company having closed its Manhattan office and transitioned all of us to working from home, I moved out of New York at the end of September, staying first for a few months in the suburban Maryland area where I had previously lived, and then moved to Florida, where we were planning to open a new office. While in Maryland I made an appointment with an orthopedic surgeon to get a second opinion on the knee. The office gave me an appointment with Craig Miller, the same doctor who had made the presentation at the running class years earlier, the one with the slides from *Younger Next Year* that showed how regular training can dramatically change the arc of a person's physical decline. When Dr. Miller walked in, I mentioned his talk and the enormous impact it had had on my life, happy to have the opportunity to thank him after so many years. We then got down to business. He had reviewed the results of my X-ray and gave me the news. I had osteoarthritis in the injured knee. I was momentarily shocked. Visions of my running being over flashed through my mind, but he assured me that I would still be able to run. He also told me that I had a lot of fluid on the knee and drained it, which provided immediate relief, and said that I could slowly resume training. I then went to see my old physical therapist, Rachel Miller, who also encouraged me to believe that I should be able to get back to marathons. I was glad to have hope that the osteoarthritis diagnosis was not, as far as my running was concerned, a death sentence and decided that I would try to be one of the success stories.

For a few weeks, it was like starting over entirely. I would run for one minute and then walk for one, a frequency of walking that I now had little patience for. Slowly, over a period of weeks, I increased the duration of the run intervals to five minutes. I was moving even more slowly than usual as my body contended with months of lost running and the extra Covid pounds, but at least I was on my way back.

CHAPTER 28

Lindsey Parry

As my return to running continued to progress. I was starting to believe Rachel Miller's assurance that I could return to marathons despite the osteoarthritis diagnosis. Perhaps even more than that would be possible. After Arizona, I had told myself that I would never again try to fit an Ironman into my busy life. While training for the 2019 race, I had to contend not just with the competing demands of work and working out but also had to allocate time for an hour and a half of commuting each day.

With my new, Covid-imposed, work-from-home routine, I no longer had a commute. That removed one of the main practical impediments to taking on another Ironman, and I started to think seriously about a second one. It would give me something long-range to plan and train for, which I was sure would help with the low-level, constant pressure of life in a Covid-restricted world. I was also excited about the prospect of applying my "magic of two" philosophy to Ironman. And as much as anything, I wanted to return, however briefly, to that Superman feeling that I had experienced during the final months of training for Arizona.

In 2019, Ironman had been an aspirational goal race for me and also, I had hoped, a qualifier for a second attempt at Comrades. I had persuaded myself that even though I would be 58 by the time of Comrades 2020, I might still have enough in the tank to finish what I had started. Now I again reconsidered what might be possible. For the 2022 edition of Comrades, I would be 60 and yet, at the same time, far more experienced than I had been in 2018. With 2020 drawing to a close and vaccines on the horizon, I was confident that 2021 would bring with it a renewal of racing. I decided to re-run my 2020 Comrades plan. I would again do Ironman Arizona as a qualifier (this time in November 2021) and then pivot to Comrades training for June of 2022.[2]

To further improve my chances at a successful Comrades finish, I decided that I would work with a coach who had substantial experience with this specific race, which meant working with someone based in South Africa. I immediately thought of Lindsey Parry, having listened to his podcast for years. The training plan that I had downloaded and followed in 2018 was one that Lindsey had created as part of his responsibilities as the official coach for Comrades. I had always found Lindsey compelling. In addition to his seemingly encyclopedic knowledge of all things running, he had an attitude that I found an appealing combination of what could often be coaching opposites, can-do and aspirational on the one hand and sensitive and empathetic

---

2. A few months later, Comrades 2022 as delayed by three months to August.

on the other. Though I assumed Lindsey would not be available, I knew that he had a team of coaches working with him, and I focused on signing up with one of them. Just as I was poised to do that, the remarkable happened. With racing on hold, Lindsey had experienced his own wave of cancellations as runners had nothing specific to train for. I saw an email indicating that, for the first time in years, he had some available slots.

I signed up the day I saw the email, determined to get in before others beat me to it. During one of our first sessions, held over Skype, I laid out my plan for an Ironman in 2021 as a Comrades qualifier, to be followed by Comrades 2022. I knew I couldn't be ready in time for a June 2021 Comrades which, in any event, I had assumed would be an up-run. Lindsey agreed that I should focus on the down-run because, given my history, I would likely need those precious extra minutes. He also liked the idea of again using Ironman as a qualifier. Though I hadn't been aware of it from his Podcasts, Lindsey was an Ironman himself and was one of the coaches of South Africa's Olympic triathlon team. I was in the right hands.

Over the following weeks, Lindsey looked at all aspects of my training for places to tweak. He was a proponent of run-training based in part on heart rate zones, which meant that I needed to start wearing a chest strap heart rate monitor for my runs so that he could structure those workouts more accurately. He also wanted to institute power-based training zones for my spin bike training. It took a few weeks of experimentation, but once we were dialed in, the quality of those sessions dramatically improved. The swim was a different story. After examining a month or so of data on a variety of different swim workouts, Lindsey gave me his verdict. He could see that adding volume was not really going to make much of a difference. If I wanted to improve my swim speed, I would really need to work on technique. That was something, of course, he could not teach me over Skype. The hard truth was that the best thing I could do for my triathlon training was to reduce the number of weekly swim sessions and allocate the time to biking or running.

We agreed that I should target a 70.3 for a few months before Arizona, and I chose one scheduled for the end of August in Maine. As that race drew nearer, I decided to get a new fitting for my tri bike, worried that my botched reassembly for Arizona had thrown things off. I decided to go to a local bike shop for the adjustment. I wanted to get it done before Maine so that I could test it there and then approach Arizona with complete confidence in my bike set-up. The process took over an hour and seemed rigorous. Still, I continued to train exclusively on the spin bike and only managed to take the tri bike outside for a single 45-minute ride before the race.

We were near the end of racing season for the northeast, and the temperatures for race day were going to be in the 60s, which would be ideal for the bike and the run. The swim would be in the ocean. The water temperature was forecast to be around 73, much colder than my pool swims but nearly ten degrees warmer than Arizona. Having survived the Arizona swim, a ten-degree cushion sounded luxurious. Race morning in Maine found me standing on the beach with the other racers, Orlie watching from the side. I seeded myself in the section for a 43-46-minute estimated swim time, the range for both of my Atlantic City swims, and patiently waited for the start. During check-in the day before, they had announced that the water temperature was 68, five degrees below normal. It would still be above Arizona, and, even if it felt cold, I now knew the secret—just keep plunging your head in until it stays.

The race began, and the line of swimmers snaked toward the start area. When it was my turn, I waded forward through small waves until the water was above my waist and then started to swim. I put my head in the water, and it was AZ all over again—gasping, hyperventilating, racing heart rate. No problem, I thought. I just need to keep at it, and soon it will all be fine. But I couldn't get my head to stay, and I just couldn't slow my breathing or my heart rate. I was doing a mix of freestyle with my head entirely out of the water and breaststroke, trying every few feet to dunk my head in. Each time it was the same result. With the physical struggle came the emotional negativity. I wondered why I was putting myself through this, how I would be able to do Arizona in three months, and what a bummer it was that Orlie was watching and that so many other people knew I was doing this race today, which meant that I could never simply quit and walk away. I knew I would get through it as I had in Arizona, but it still felt like hell.

The swim course had three sections: a straight "out," followed by a 90 degree turn that would take us parallel to the shore, and then a second 90 degree turn that would bring us back to the beach. As I was getting closer to the first turn, I still wasn't in a normal rhythm and started to worry that the 70-minute cut-off for the swim leg might be in play. Not long after I made the first turn, I started to improve but was still mixing in a lot of breaststroke. It wasn't until the final section that I got grooved and was finally able to do a normal, consistent freestyle.

When I finally reached shallow water at the end of the course, I stood and unsteadily made my way to the beach. I felt dizzy, my legs were wobbly, and I had a strong desire to just lie down and regroup. I knew I couldn't do that. Orlie was there, and I didn't want to scare her. I was also afraid that medical staff would come over and pull me from the race. I wasn't sure where the pad was to officially end the swim. I hit my watch where I thought it might be and it showed 47 minutes. It was the slowest of my three 70.3 swim legs but not as slow as I had imagined when I was out there struggling. Still, I left the swim dismayed at how much I had struggled with the cold and concerned about what that might mean for Arizona.

When I got to transition, I made my way to my bike, peeled off my wetsuit bottoms and started to get myself organized. Over loudspeakers, I heard Simon & Garfunkel singing "Feelin Groovy" and had to laugh at the part about slowing down and not moving too fast, which lightened my mood. I walked out of transition, got on the bike, and started pedaling. I had pushed away most of the bad feeling from the swim. I was only a few minutes behind my projected swim time, and I was confident I could still turn in good performances on the bike and the run. Perhaps I would be able to break three hours on the bike, something that I had come within seconds of doing during my second

Atlantic City 70.3. As for the run, Lindsey wanted to see me break 2:20, and I was determined to get as close to that as I could, though I thought his "B" goal of a sub-2:30 was more realistic.

As the ride began, I kept moving back and forth between sitting upright on the bike and tucked in the Aero position, but something just didn't feel right. At one point, while in Aero, I went to take a drink from the bottle that was mounted between the bars but found that the straw was hitting my neck rather than my mouth. I must have mounted the bottle backwards, I thought, and decided to pull over and fix it. When I checked, I discovered the bottle was oriented properly after all. At that moment, I realized that my bike fitting had been a bust and that, at a minimum, the fitter had moved the bars (and with them the bottle) too close to my body. I thought I had sensed that something might be amiss during my one short trial ride. It had seemed like my knees had been close to hitting my elbows, but I had assumed that it was just because I hadn't ridden in Aero in almost two years.

The ride was scenic and mildly hilly, but I couldn't stay in Aero and couldn't hold a good speed. Over time, it seemed to be more of a casual, sightseeing ride than a race. I hadn't asked Lindsey about pre-race nutrition and had instead followed Don Fink's advice for Arizona from two years earlier, which had me drinking two bottles of Gatorade before entering the water. That was on top of a large flask of coffee that I had consumed during a nearly one-hour car ride to the race site that morning. As I rode, frustrated at having to constantly shift between sitting upright and brief stints in Aero, I now had the additional problem that I was way over-hydrated. The entire ride I was either desperately needing to pee or was in the process of slowing down so I could actually pee. All of that only added to my sense that the bike leg was a lost cause. My one consolation was that the course mile markers were way ahead of my GPS. At a point that my bike computer said was only mile 54, I saw the bike finish, and suddenly, mercifully, it was over.

I racked my bike and checked my time. At 3:32 it was more than half an hour slower than at Atlantic City in 2019. It was another bad leg and another disappointment. I could see that some runners were already heading to the finish, only about a half mile away. That only added to my increasingly negative view about the race, with a half marathon still to go. I walked toward the exit, preoccupied with my disappointing swim and bike legs. But if I could turn in a good performance on the run, I decided, the day would not be a total bust.

A few miles in I saw that I was running just above a 12-minute per mile pace, good enough to beat my second Atlantic City run leg but well off Lindsey's "B" race goal of 2:30. I couldn't summon up the intensity to push myself harder. Instead, I told myself I would see how I felt later in the race and turn it up then if I felt up to it. My pace stayed consistent as I ticked off the miles. My body felt fine; the day had been far more of an emotional struggle than a physical one. As I reached the final turn toward the finish, with about a mile still to go, I checked my watch. It showed that I was at a little over 2:28, which meant that even a sub-2:40 run might be out of reach. I decided to go full tilt until the end, skipping my final walk breaks and hoping to extract some small victory from the race. I kept pounding away and looked at my watch as I crossed. I had just missed breaking 2:40, the day's final disappointment.

CHAPTER 29

The Iceman

Except for the brief flash of exertion during the final mile of the run, it had been a dispiriting showing. I would have to sort out its implications for Arizona and, beyond that, for Comrades. Given how well my training had been going, I had expected the race to be a confidence-builder, that I would set new PRs in at least two and perhaps all three legs. Instead, I was left with significant concerns about all of them. With the swim, my fears about another cold shock episode were now heightened. My struggle in the water in Maine had gone on much longer than in Arizona, despite the fact that the water was five degrees warmer. It was clear that I had not truly figured out how to deal with the cold. For the bike, my set-up was a disaster, and unless I addressed it before Arizona, it had the potential to destroy my entire race.

As for the run, my inability to dig deep and run faster was perhaps the least of my troubles. It wasn't my worst run performance in a 70.3. Still, the fact that I had not been able to turn in the type of time that Lindsey had thought I was capable of triggered a different anxiety. A few months earlier I had turned 59, and, in the back of my mind, I had always known that eventually my ability to improve as a racer would come to an end. Invariably, at some point, I could expect to see my times get slower. In those heady first years of running, when I was reading everything about the sport that I could get my hands on, I came across something that had really stuck with me. It was one coach's observation that everyone, regardless of when they start running, could look forward to ten years of improvement, after which they could expect to see their times get progressively slower. It had been a source of comfort during those first years when, even though I was in my 50's, I was able to keep getting stronger, year after year turning in faster times and completing longer distances. But I had started running in earnest in the summer of 2010—the Veterans Day 10K had been in November of that year—and by the time of the Maine 70.3 in August 2021, my ten years were up.

Of course, I knew that the 10-year observation wasn't an ironclad rule. I had also read stories about runners who made changes to their training after decades in the sport and who then unexpectedly experienced speed improvements. Still, getting slower with age is the eventual destiny of all runners. The point at which my slowing would begin was, I feared, now upon me. Given that my finish at IMAZ in 2019 was with only a one hour and sixteen-minute cushion, I hated the idea that during my upcoming Ironman I might have to spend long hours worrying, as I had at Comrades in 2018, about whether I would be cut before reaching the finish line. I pushed all that aside as much as I could.

Certainly, the eternally positive Lindsey had no sense of foreboding about my ability to do Ironman or Comrades at my age. We focused on trying to address the weaknesses that Maine had exposed—among other things dropping a swim session and replacing it with an additional bike workout. Those were straightforward coaching fixes. But sorting out the bike set-up and the cold shock were not things that I could look to Lindsey to handle.

For the bike, I needed to get re-fit. I had no desire to go back to the same person who had so clearly botched things before Maine. I did some research and came across a former professional cyclist named Steffi who had a studio in her house. I went to see her and was dazzled by the array of sophisticated equipment. The process ended up taking nearly an entire day, but in the end, I finally felt confident that my bike set-up was right. Just to make sure, I resolved that I would do the rest of my bike training with my tri bike mounted on a trainer, rather than on the more comfortable spin bike, to give me as many hours as possible in Aero.

The swim was a different challenge. In Arizona in 2019 I had toughed it out and, within less than a minute or so, overcome the cold and gone on to have a great swim. In Maine, the struggle with the cold had gone on much longer, and it had put me in a funk that carried over to the entire rest of the race. It seemed to have all been a matter of chance, which provided no basis for confidence about how the upcoming swim would go. And then, out of the blue, a potential solution presented itself. I stumbled across a podcast interview with a guy who had become proficient in the "Wim Hof" method, named after a remarkable

Dutch man who was a proponent of ice baths and other cold exposure as a means for providing all manner of health and performance benefits. I did some additional research, and it really did seem to make sense.

For me, living in South Florida at the time, the exposure would have to come through cold showers. I started to experiment, turning the water temperature down at the end of the shower, slowly increasing the duration and the amount of temperature drop over a period of weeks until I was taking 45-second cold showers at the lowest possible temperature. Over time, I could see the power of what Wim Hof was promoting. A blast of cold water that previously triggered a gasp and a sharp escalation in my heart rate and breathing lost most of its power over me. I could now focus on deep and consistent breathing while simply noting the coldness of the water, without letting it overwhelm me. This being Florida, a cold shower was still likely slightly above the expected water temperature in Arizona but, I hoped, the training could be just the thing to get me past the fear of another cold shock episode.

CHAPTER 30

Return to Arizona

In the final weeks before the race, I emerged from the negativity that Maine had triggered. I felt good about the new bike set-up and my cold water preparation. In addition, having already done one Ironman, I was confident that I was up to the challenge. I arrived in Arizona determined not just to finish but also to turn in a faster time than I had in 2019.

For the prior race, I had stayed miles away from the race venue. This time, I chose a nearby hotel that was within walking distance. I liked the idea of not having to drive and park on race morning. An additional benefit was being constantly surrounded by other racers. Everyone was excited about the race and eager to talk about it. It was great to again be in that environment, among people who understood what the training and the race were all about. Those who had done Ironman before invariably had great stories to tell. As for the first-timers, their anticipation and anxiety were a reminder of the swirl of emotions I had felt two years earlier. Now, I was in the happy position of being able to provide reassurance to the newbies.

I headed over to registration and then to the race briefing. As they put up course maps, I realized that the direction of the swim had been reversed from 2019. I couldn't decide if this was a good thing or bad thing, though Orlie pointed out that given that I breathe on my left side, sighting the buoys, which would be on my right, could be an issue. For the rest of the day, I went through the other pre-race tasks that had occupied me in 2019, taking into account my problems from the prior race. For the bike, I arranged my Gatorade bottles so that I could do the filling before the race started and also planned on carrying two brand-new inflaters as well as the trusty hand-pump that had saved my 2019 race. For the run, I made sure to include a long-sleeved shirt to avoid the tough battle with plummeting temperatures that had so plagued me the last time.

Now that the race was nearly upon me, I felt my confidence about the swim beginning to slip. I hoped that my Wim Hof reading and cold showers would get me through the first brutal minutes in the water without panic, but I wasn't sure. I noticed that there was a practice swim scheduled for the next day, something I had skipped in 2019. I resolved to go and see if I had figured anything out, realizing that it would only reinforce my fears if it went badly. In addition to experiencing the water, I also thought I could talk to other racers and see if anyone had a helpful suggestion.

There was a huge turnout for the practice swim. While I was putting on my wetsuit, I chatted with a guy with a large dot-M tattoo on his shoulder. The Ironman tattoo is everywhere at these races, but this one was unusual. The M portion had 12 tiles, which I asked about. He explained that as he finished each Ironman (this would be his fourth or fifth) he would fill in another tile. When he got to 12, he would be able to go to the World Championships in Hawaii on Ironman's legacy program. That race would fill the dot and complete the tattoo. Since he clearly was experienced, I took the opportunity to ask about acclimating to the cold water. He told me to just go slow: "take as much time as you need and hold onto a kayak if you need to." That made sense and I resolved to follow his advice.

The race organizers had set up a 350-yard loop course. I got in line with the others to enter the water. When it was my turn, I began with a slow walk before slowly transitioning to swimming. I started with breaststroke and then switched to freestyle, all the while deep breathing. I had to pull my face out of the water the first few times but without a sense of panic. Within a short while I was swimming normally and completed the loop. I avoided cold shock, but my energy had been low and, as at Maine, I felt dizzy as I got out of the water. I wasn't sure what that was all about and still couldn't shake my anxiety. My worrying intensified over the rest of the day and into the night. I was able to get to bed early but woke up multiple times. With each wake-up, the anxious thoughts resumed. It wasn't just the continuing worry about the swim. From my experience in 2019, I had no illusions about what the next day would bring. It would be long and brutal and the anticipation of it was agonizing.

On race morning, a bunch of us filled the sidewalks as we walked toward the race venue, all holding morning clothes bags. I got to my bike, checked to make sure the tires were still inflated, put on the two bottles with Gatorade, installed the bike computer, and pulled on my wetsuit bottom. Using our phones, Orlie and I quickly found each other and headed to the swim start, where I lined up alongside the 1:31-1:40 group. In general people around me were upbeat—excited about the day getting started and not yet in the throes of the battle. Orlie and I had a final hug. Then, she went off to position herself to take pictures. The cannon went off, and the crowd started to inch forward. I realized as I drew closer to the water that Mike Reilly was broadcasting from inside the corral, wearing a hat that said "IM #200," signifying that this would be the 200th race he was calling. He was high-fiving swimmers as they walked by, and I was excited to give him a high five also.

Before I knew it, we were split into lanes, with volunteers guiding one row of swimmers at a time to move forward. Soon, it was my row's turn. I walked forward slowly, as suggested by the guy with the tile tattoo, and eased into the water. I started with a mix of freestyle with my head out and breaststroke as I navigated the immediate area out of the start, which included an early turn to the right. I eased my face in and out a few times while breathing out, as I moved from breaststroke to freestyle, and within less than a minute I was able to comfortably submerge my face and stroke normally. What a difference from 2019—and, to my relief, a great start to the swim.

As the swim got underway, I found that I did have some trouble sighting as Orlie had predicted and was a little too far to the left most of the time. I didn't really mind though. I was going straight enough, and I liked being in less-crowded water. I also realized that the change in course direction provided a huge benefit. As I turned to my left to breathe, I found myself looking at the nearby side of the lake, rather than toward the middle as in 2019, and the buildings and other landmarks along the shore gave me a constant sense of progress. My one worry as I progressed through the first long stretch toward a distant bridge was whether I had pressed start on my Garmin before entering the water. I couldn't remember having done it.

I reached the end of the first long straightaway, crossed to the other side of the lake, and turned again to head back in the other direction. I continued to swim well, with my watch as my only concern. I finally picked up the red buoy that would turn us to the left, back to shore. I covered the final short distance to the exit and got out of the water. I was elated. The swim was done, and there had been no panic. I was also able to immediately stand as I came out of the water and wasn't dizzy. After removing my wetsuit, I trotted toward transition, glancing down at my watch. I was dismayed to see it read 0:00. I really had forgotten to start it, a watch I had spent more than $600 on just a few weeks earlier for its long battery life, specifically for this race in order to address yet another mistake from 2019.

I heard a voice from the side and saw my nephew Andy and his girlfriend, Becca, who lived in the area. I asked Andy what time it was – he said 9:02. I had seen a race clock just before I entered the water and had noticed the time – 7:24. Assuming I had gone into the water a minute or so later and eaten up a few minutes taking off the wet suit, I had probably completed the swim in around 1:30. I had harbored some thoughts about crushing my earlier swim time, but I had focused most of my mental energy on just getting through it without panic and had achieved that. Then I heard Orlie's voice and saw her. I told her the swim had gone well and kept moving toward transition.

CHAPTER 31

Personally Victimized

I retrieved my transition bag and changed for the bike leg. I found my bike, turned on the bike computer, headed to the exit, and mounted at the line. I saw Orlie, Andy, and Becca again as I got on the bike. Within moments, I was out of the chute and on the road. The first stretch went well. Aero felt good, and my speed was comfortably climbing to 16 and 17 mph. Maybe my optimistic predictions would be realized: a bike split closer to seven hours or possibly even a tad below. As we turned onto the Beeline Highway, I detected a slight uphill earlier than I had remembered, and the winds also seemed to be picking up stronger than I remembered. Since I so rarely ride outside, I wasn't sure if the wind was genuinely strong or if it was just "apparent wind" from my own bike speed. Periodically, I looked at the plant life on the side of the road. At first, everything looked still, but then I clearly saw branches moving. It was, I was now convinced, a stiffer headwind than the one I faced in 2019.

I fought my way uphill, staying mostly in Aero. At first, I thought I was on pace to beat my 1:21 time in 2019 for the first "out" segment, but the minutes kept creeping by, and I still wasn't at the end. When I finally reached the turnaround, I saw that the "out" had taken me about 1:28, seven minutes off my 2019 pace. That was nerve-wracking. I had learned the day before that they had cut 20 minutes off the standard 17-hour race cut-off, which removed a nice chunk of my cushion. That 20 minutes had come out of the time allotted for the bike; the swim and run cut-offs were standard length. Apparently, that was to ensure all racers would be off the bike course before it got dark, though I didn't understand why that wasn't an issue on more or less the same date in 2019. As I turned for the "back" segment, I was worried. If I were seven minutes slower per segment—or even just for the three uphill segments—that could really push me close to the shortened bike cutoff. And calculating precisely where I was relative to the cutoff was impossible because of my failure to start my watch when I began the swim. I kept trying to remind myself to focus only on the current "box," as I had in 2019, but this time I couldn't stop myself from doing the larger math.

I started rocketing downhill. The speed kept up far longer than I had remembered for the down stretch in 2019, and when I reached the turnaround, I saw that it had only taken about 52 minutes. I could live with 1:28 and :52 for two more loops, which would bring me in right at seven hours. That calmed my nerves a little bit. The second "out" was even more challenging than the first. The winds remained very strong and it was painfully slow to go uphill, even slower than the first time. The second downhill was a tad slower than the first but still wonderful. Upon completing it I told myself that I had two uphills under my belt. Only one to go.

I turned for the third uphill, and this time it was slower still. The winds, if anything, were stronger, and I was getting tired. I had seen someone post on Facebook a few days before the race that given the expected 80+ temperatures on race day, you really needed to be drinking—and peeing—to make sure you didn't get dehydrated on the bike. I had been drinking but had not felt the need to pee. I worried that I was getting dehydrated but just couldn't be sure. The third uphill seemed to drag on forever. All the while I was trying to do race time math, estimating a 1:30 swim, a 15-minute transition, a bike ride that seemed headed above 7.5 hours, another long transition, and then a slow run—all against a 16:40 cut-off. It seemed way too close for comfort. The last two or three miles were an eternity. Then, finally, I reached the turnaround.

At first, there was the relief of the fast initial downhill, until I realized the sun was almost directly in my eyes. My sunglasses, which should have made glare a non-issue, had a cross bar which essentially blocked my field of vision when I angled my eyes to look forward, something my indoor training had prevented me from experiencing before the race. With the unresolvable cross-bar problem, my only choice was to spend more time sitting upright, out of Aero. As I continued the final "back," I was battling fatigue from the long ride and especially the three climbs into headwinds, dehydration, pain in my wrists from spending so much time out of Aero, and dry and tired eyes from staring directly into the setting sun. I kept willing myself forward, but this was going to be the slowest of the three downhills.

We finally left the freeway and reached town for the last few miles of the ride. I just couldn't wait to get off the bike. I knew the run would be a challenge, but the combination of the wind and the sun had made for an agonizing ride. I was also now convinced that I really was dehydrated – I was starting to have cramps in my left leg which a few salt pills seemed to keep in check, but that didn't bode well for the long and slow marathon still ahead. I had been checking my time periodically and as I neared transition I saw that, despite everything, I would barely beat my 2019 bike split of about 7:30. I no longer really cared. I was just happy there had not been a complete meltdown that had driven my bike leg over eight hours, which would have had a spillover effect on the run. Orlie was there to watch me finish the bike leg and saw me nearly fall as I dismounted. It was not a confidence-inspiring moment for either of us.

As I walked toward the changing tent, I noticed a bank of porta potties just beyond it, and decided to jump in for a quick pee. I must have really looked awful because as I walked past the tent opening, a volunteer asked if I was dropping from the race. I assured her I wasn't and kept moving. Once inside the changing room, I relaxed a bit. The other guys seemed as happy as me to have the bike behind them. Everyone was talking about the headwinds and others had also struggled with the sun. I later heard the winds were 15-20 mph, which caused an attrition rate of over 20%, more than twice what was typical.

I changed, making sure to take the long-sleeve shirt from my run bag even though I was overheated and didn't feel like wearing it. I tied it around my waist and headed out. Lindsey had said to spend the first two miles taking in nutrition, doing a lot of walking, and trying to get the hips in alignment. I took it easy but felt like a wreck. It seemed to take forever to hit the mile 1 sign. The idea of a 5:40-6:15 run leg—the target that Lindsey had given me—seemed insanely ambitious. I was just too fried from the bike.

I got to mile two and was still exhausted. I had set my run-walk ratio at 6/1 but couldn't come close to running for six minutes. Lindsey wanted me to be close to a 13 minute-per-mile pace for the first two miles, but I was not hitting that either.

I periodically checked my pace and saw that I was in the 14:25 minute-per-mile (MPM) range. That was way off my target, but I was relieved. If I could keep it below 15 MPM, it would not be pretty, but I could finish. I was still experimenting with my run/walk ratio and by mile 8 was moving toward one minute running followed by 30 seconds walking. My pace actually improved to 14:05 MPM, which was encouraging. As I moved through the data screens on my watch, I saw that my heart rate was regularly reaching as high as 200, which I assumed was artificially high "cardiac drift" brought on by fatigue and dehydration, rather than a sign that I was truly redlining. It made me nervous, however. I was depleted, light-headed, and just wasn't sure I could hold it together. I wouldn't quit just because it was painful and uncomfortable, but I wasn't sure I could physically continue to function. I had an especially low moment when I did the math at an estimated 15:00 MPM at the 8-mile mark and realized that 18 miles left in the run meant another four and a half hours of this.

The route was a little different from 2019. There were now three loops instead of two, which itself was an emotional blow. Even though I was pretty sure I was only dealing with cardiac drift, part of the reason I wanted to shorten my run segments was to bring my heart rate down and in general stabilize myself. It seemed to help. I was drinking lots of water, took in a few salt pills, and eventually shifted to Gatorade as I worried that I might not be taking in enough calories. I was depleted but functioning. At mile 13, for the first time on the run, I finally felt like I was no longer at risk of unraveling physically.

I continued to churn out the miles. I saw Orlie at one point—and Andy and Becca several times—which was always a boost. Taped to a light post on the side of the course, I saw the best sign of the day: "Smile if you feel personally victimized by the headwinds on Beeline." That about summed it up.

I really wanted to keep my speed below 15 MPM for as long as possible. I felt that if I eventually cratered and needed to shift to walking only, I wanted to have built up a cushion that would be sufficient to absorb an even slower, walking-only pace. It would be easier to fight now to hang on to my current pace rather than trying, later in the run at a time when I would be even more depleted, to go faster, increase the length of my run intervals—or both.

When I got to mile 18, I began to relax. My strategy of keeping my pace below 15 MPM was holding and the math in my head was telling me that I was building up a safe cushion, one that would have me finish perhaps as much as an hour ahead of the cut off. That meant that I could switch to a 100% walk for the last few miles and still be fine, which was exactly the kind of insurance I had been looking for.

I finally reached the mile 20 marker and knew that it was just a matter of churning it out. Miles 21, 22, 23, and then 24 went by comfortably, with the quiet, the darkness, and the city lights off in the distance creating a pleasant backdrop as I savored the thought that I really would be able to finish a second Ironman, and to do so after my 59th birthday. I was surprised to see Becca and Andy just before mile 24. They greeted me warmly, but I could not get an intelligible response out, just kind of an "argh," which must have sounded insane. Soon after, I was able to hear Mike Reilly's voice in the background—a welcome sound, a beacon calling me home. At mile 26, the route split and I made the long-anticipated turn to the right for the finish.

It was a beautiful finish area with dazzling sparklers going off on either side as I ran through, but my only feeling was one of relief. I looked forward and back to space myself better than I had in 2019, when I had run right up on the guy finishing ahead of me, and jogged through with my head forward, smiling grimly, arms churning. Thrilled as I was to be finishing, I just couldn't muster the energy to raise my hands in triumph.

I heard Mike Reilly calling out the names of the finishers, together with the iconic "You are an Ironman." This was it. I would really savor it this time. When he got to me, I heard "Jeffrey Weiss, from New York City, trains in Central Park." Then he was on to the next one. He had actually forgotten to give me the "You are an Ironman" line. I had to laugh, but if it had been my first and presumably only finish, I imagine I would have had a very different reaction to being denied my benediction.

CHAPTER 32

And He's an Old Guy

As I left the finisher's area I saw that Orlie, Andy and Becca—now joined by my brother Mark and his daughter Madison—were there to greet me. It was a different feeling than in 2019. Then I had been amazed that I had pulled it off. This time it was more complicated. My dominant emotion was one of relief. It easily could have gone the other way, with a DNF and a sad story to tell about headwinds and dehydration. I had avoided that and felt, much more so than in 2019, that I had really earned this finish. When I look at a post-race picture that I took with Orlie, I am struck by how tortured my face looks, as though I have just had a brush with something terrifying.

I checked my statistics on the race app. It was nice to see that both my run and bike legs were slightly faster than in 2019. But because my swim and transitions had been slower, my total time of 15:53:43 was about seven minutes behind that of 2019, though at least still below 16 hours. Of course, the crucial thing was that I had finished. Over the next hours, as the rest of the field either finished or dropped, the app kept updating. For my age group, only 152 out of 196 who started would go on to complete the race. When I realized that nearly a quarter of the guys in my age group didn't finish, I really felt like I had dodged a bullet. At the airport a few days later, we met a 30-something South African wearing an IMAZ shirt who was also waiting to board the same flight. When we got off the plane, the stewardess, who had apparently earlier told the pilot that the South African had just done the Ironman, told him that I had, too. I didn't hear it, but Orlie did: the pilot had responded, "And he's an old guy!" Indeed, I am.

Over the next few days, I thought a lot about the race and what finishing it had meant to me. I was extraordinarily happy to have done two, which made me feel more able to authentically call myself an "Ironman." I was particularly happy about the swim experience. I felt that I had identified a major problem with cold water from my Arizona and Maine races and then, with the Wim Hof breathing, cold shower experimentation, and practice swim the day before the race, been able to address it. One of the ways in which I have justified my participation in a time-consuming sport like Ironman is that I believe that I am getting tangible things out of it that can help me in other spheres of my life. This really had been a translatable experience: recognizing that I had a limitation that was holding me back and then finding and implementing a solution that allowed me to overcome it.

The bike, and the long and slow run that followed it, left me with a different feeling. I was proud that I had toughed it out on the bike despite the headwinds and dehydration.

I also felt good that I had soldiered on during the run even though I really hadn't been sure I could finish until about mile 13. Still, my bike riding skills were sorely lacking. I was too marginal of a rider to do an Ironman race with supreme confidence that I had everything under control and it was all routine – in the way that I now feel about finishing a marathon. If I were ever to do another Ironman, I concluded, improving my cycling fitness would be at the top of my list of things to address.

A few days after IMAZ, I had my next Skype session with Lindsey. I had been dreading it since my run split had been so far off the target he had set for me. I wasn't sure what to expect and was worried that he might tell me to write off Comrades. In the end, it was a long, fascinating session, classic Lindsey. We talked at length about the race: the high attrition rate, the uphill bike sections into strong headwinds, and the cardiac drift. Lindsey pointed out that uphill cycling uses the same muscles as running, which clearly had an impact on my run. He also explained that if you get dehydrated on the bike, which I apparently had, you really can't catch it up during the marathon leg. He said my 60/30 run/walk strategy had been the right call to bring my heart rate down and blood pressure up to get rid of the dizziness. On balance, he believed that taking out the very first and last parts of the run, I had for the most part done what I would need to do for Comrades. He said we couldn't look at it as a success, but there were "a lot of good elements" and in the scheme of things I hadn't done too badly.

Lindsey then mapped out the next few months of training. I would take one week completely off followed by one week of non-impact exercise. Then, I would train easily for two weeks followed by an 8-week training cycle with the goal of running a 10K at what had previously been my 5K pace. After that, I would have another 8-week training cycle, this time with the goal of running a half marathon at my new 10K pace. Next would be a 10-week cycle in preparation for a full marathon, which he wanted me to run in under 4:50. Though I had qualified with my Ironman finish, he wanted to see me run a qualifying marathon as well, to remove any "gremlins" that I might still have about my ability to finish Comrades within the cut-off. By the end of the session, it was clear. My Comrades quest was still on.

CHAPTER 33

Who is Going to Beat You Up?

While I was glad to still be working toward a return to Comrades, and while I trusted Lindsey completely, I had never liked speedwork and was not looking forward to taking on the series of challenges that he had laid out for me. I found the breathlessness that I experienced during fast running uncomfortable, and it was a mental struggle to endure that for any length of time. Still, I couldn't argue with Lindsey's logic. Clearly, my cruising speed needed to get faster if I were going to have any real chance at finishing Comrades, and I trusted Lindsay's plan to increase my speed over progressively longer distances, beginning with the 10K.

With the time frame that Lindsey laid out, I went online to look for races that would fit my schedule. For the half and full marathons, I found good candidates: the New York City Half Marathon in March and the Manitoba Marathon in June. Both would be on favorable courses, and in weather conditions that should be mild. The 10K was a different matter. I didn't want to travel any significant distance for a 10K and I couldn't find a suitable one within driving distance of my apartment. We resolved that, instead, I would run my own 10K on the 3-mile bike/pedestrian loop where I did most of my run training.

In January, it was time. We had agreed on 10-minute/30-second run-walk intervals. Lindsey wanted me to break one hour, something I hadn't tried to do in a decade. It was about as tough as I thought it would be. Through the first four intervals, I stayed within the target pace but was unable to simply settle into a rhythm and feel confident that I would break an hour. During my fifth interval, a woman up ahead who was looking in my direction put up her hands to ask me to stop. I assumed she wanted to ask the time or for directions, and I raced by her, blurting out that I was doing a time trial so that she would understand that I had seen her and was not being purposely rude. In response she called out, "So, then he will beat me up!"

I stopped, walked back to her, and asked, "Who is going to beat you up?"

She pointed at a guy who was walking toward us from about 40 feet away. I stood with her, watching him as he approached and then walked past, never breaking stride and never engaging with either of us. I didn't know what had happened previously, but he certainly did not seem to be pursuing a further confrontation. After he was about 20 feet away, I suggested that she go in the opposite direction. She confirmed that was her plan, and I was off again. When I hit 6.2 miles, I stopped my Garmin and checked my time:

59:00. I had done it, even with the lost time on the path. More satisfying was the knowledge that I wouldn't have to do it again. I still would need to do a fast half and a fast full, and those would be even more difficult. But, at least, this distance could be checked off.

The next session with Lindsey was a pleasure. He told me that he was "chuffed" with the time. He explained that it converted to a 2:10 half (though he thought something between 2:12 and 2:13 was more likely) and a 4:28 full (with Lindsey thinking a 4:35 more likely). Those targets seemed shockingly ambitious to me. Both would be PRs and the marathon in particular by a significant margin over my prior best time of 4:46. But Lindsey was supremely confident. He assured me that we were "well on track for our ultimate goal of finishing Comrades."

Over the next months, I continued to put in the miles as my focus shifted to the New York City Half Marathon. It follows the last 13 miles of the New York Marathon and is a popular race. The lottery to enter had finished months before I picked it out, and my only option was to sign up with a charity. I tried to find something that had relevance to my life and ultimately chose Team World Vegan. I actually *was* a vegan, having become one more than eight years earlier after a co-worker sent me a link to a Ted Talk by Rip Esselstyn, a fireman and former professional triathlete. I had been bothered by my eating habits and weight for a long time, but had been unable to find any kind of solution. Three years into my new fitness journey—even after my first marathon and multiple triathlons—I still weighed over 220. My new seriousness about training brought into stark relief the fact that my weight issues were tied to food rather than to any lack of physical activity.

Esselstyn's talk was captivating, making a great case for the health benefits of a vegan diet. I followed that up with some reading on the subject and was sold. It was not just the physical benefits; it also struck me that this was a lifestyle that I could permanently integrate into my life, rather than a diet involving uncomfortable, short-term changes with which I would inevitably struggle. Within six months of the switch, I had dropped over 20 pounds—just in time for my second marathon—and had been able to keep it off for years. That was not the only physical change. My cholesterol had dropped nearly 40 points, and I had more energy. Running with Team World Vegan was a nice opportunity to recognize the positive impact veganism had had on my life.

The Wednesday before New York, Lindsey told me that he wanted me to target a 2:10-2:12 finish, with 2:15 being my worst case. That meant a per mile pace of ideally 9:49-10:00, but no slower than 10:18. That seemed hard to imagine given the much slower pace of my long runs, and I was really feeling the pressure. I knew that I needed to hit Lindsey's target to stay on track for a fast marathon and, from there, to have a realistic shot at a Comrades finish.

As the race got underway, I realized that given Lindsey's pace target of around 10 minutes per mile, I could use the mile markers as a kind of pace bracelet, checking my elapsed time as I reached each one (one mile, ten minutes; two miles, 20 minutes; three miles, 30 minutes, etc.). At each of the first six markers I checked the elapsed time, and each time I was slightly ahead of ten minutes per mile. At mile 7, I had a bit of a letdown. I started to think ahead and realized that I still had a long way to go. Fortunately, the emotional low didn't last for long. When I got to mile 10, I felt like I had done the work, wasn't breaking down, and just needed to hold on. My pace had slowed slightly, but I was still in range. At mile 11, based on my math, I calculated that I could run each of the last two miles one minute slower than my target pace and still get in under 2:15. That was a huge boost, and I kept pushing.

We ran through Times Square and then uptown, toward Central Park. Soon after getting into the park, where the crowds were especially thick, we ran past a series of distance markers: 800 yards to go, then 400, then 200, and then the finish was in sight. I crossed, stopping my watch, and was delighted to see it at 2:11:50. I had done it—a new PR, more than two minutes faster than my time at the Icebreaker Half two years earlier.

I was immensely relieved to have nailed Lindsey's target. I had done so despite the course being crowded throughout, which made passing a constant feature of the race. On the other hand, it had been a pretty flat course, and the weather had been perfect. I knew that a June marathon would likely present more challenging weather conditions, and the course profile at Comrades would be anything but flat. As satisfying as the New York finish had been, I still had a lot of work ahead before I could approach Comrades with confidence in a successful finish.

CHAPTER 34

The Sun Is Following You

After a 1-week reverse-taper, the training picked right back up. Two weeks after New York, I completed a 2-hour 40-minute long run, and a few days after that was again running intervals. Every Wednesday I had my Skype sessions with Lindsey, and, week after week, it was all going smoothly. During one of our sessions, Lindsey asked how my body was handling all the training. "Totally fine," I told him.

A couple of days later I wondered whether I had given the correct answer. Though I hadn't missed a workout, I had been feeling increasing tenderness in the heel of my left foot. It was uncomfortable to put weight on it when I got out of bed in the morning, and I had taken to positioning recovery sandals so that I could step right into them when I got up. But once I laced up my running shoes, everything felt fine and it certainly never interfered with a workout, so I hadn't given it much thought.

The next week I described the situation to Lindsey. He thought I might have plantar fasciitis and suggested that I start icing it. He also recommended a series of foot exercises. I iced it a couple of times, which seemed to help, but found it hard to stick to the exercises. Still, I didn't overly stress about it. The heel situation just wasn't getting in the way of my training. In the second week of May I was doing an intervals session on my usual loop course when I suddenly felt a sharp pain in my left heel. I tried to ignore it, but it destroyed my speed. I couldn't come close to the target pace, and I also couldn't maintain proper running form. I shut down the workout. I thought a couple of days of rest and regular icing would do the trick, but each day it only seemed to get worse. Even walking was intensely painful. Unable to resolve it on my own, I scheduled an appointment with an orthopedist.

The doctor examined me, x-rayed the foot, and confirmed Lindsey's suspicion that it was plantar. He recommended icing and calf stretches and also told me that a cortisone shot might help if I was up for it. I was in favor of anything that might allow me to quickly resume training. I got in position and waited for the shot, expecting the typical brief discomfort that one feels when a needle goes in. What I got instead was an intense bolt of agony right up through the injured heel that made me gasp and involuntarily move my whole body. Still, I was happy to have done it and hopeful that it would get me back on track.

With each passing day, the pain receded until finally, after about a week, I felt ready to try a short, slow run. It felt pretty good. I could still tell that something wasn't quite right with the foot, but I was able to run. Lindsey re-structured my workouts, eliminating intervals and shortening my Sunday long runs. I had missed two four-hour runs between the time of the injury and my return, and that was worrying.

For the next few weeks, I continued to train, slowly building up the length of my runs but still playing catch-up as the Manitoba Marathon approached. Before the injury, I had been really excited about the race. The course was said to be perfectly flat, and the temperatures promised to be in the mid-60's. Lindsey had consistently been talking about a new marathon PR: smashing through the 4:50 qualifying time and potentially breaking 4:30. With each passing week of reduced training, it was becoming clear that I would not be in condition for any of that. I needed the race to complete my training, I would also need a 50K Comrades long run a month or so later, but for qualifying purposes, I would have to fall back on the Ironman finish. The confidence boost from a qualifying marathon time—the elimination of the "gremlins" that Lindsey had talked about a few months earlier—was now off the table.

Beginning ten days before Manitoba, I started to check the long-term weather forecast. To my surprise, the temperatures for race day and the days around it were projected to reach the high 80s or low 90s. I discussed it with Lindsey. He had already cautioned me to expect Manitoba to trigger a short-term return of the plantar, and the idea of traveling to Canada, having a miserable experience in blistering hot weather while running a slow marathon and re-injuring my foot, was decidedly unappealing. I looked online and saw that there was a marathon a week after Manitoba in the Seattle area called "The Super Marathon," which billed itself as "one of fastest marathon courses in the country." As the race website described it: "Enjoy 26.2 miles of scenic downhill with gorgeous views of the Cascade Mountains as you glide down the gravel trail on this point to point course" (*Super Marathon/Half Marathon*, 2024). The temperatures were also typically mild, and it all sounded far more inviting than Manitoba. Lindsey agreed that the change made sense.

With that, my temperature gaze shifted to Seattle where, to my amazement, I started to also see a forecast of unseasonably hot weather. Beginning a few days before the scheduled start, the race organizers sent out emails warning about the potential for high temperatures for the second half of the race, when it was expected to climb into the 80s and potentially into the 90s. As unpleasant as that sounded, I was not tempted to bail. I had already missed enough workouts, had already skipped one marathon because of heat, and felt that time was running out on my Comrades training. When I told Lindsey about the heat warnings, he joked: "The sun is following you." He agreed with the decision to just go ahead and do the race, come what may. Given the friendly profile of the course, Lindsey thought I might still have a shot at a Comrades qualifying time of sub-4:50, and we planned the pacing accordingly. A lot would depend on just how hot it ultimately got and how well the foot held up.

I stayed in a suburb of Seattle and, early on race morning, drove some 50 miles to the scenic area where the race would start. It was as nice as the website described it. I picked up my bib and got myself organized. Aside from the usual race necessities, I was also carrying a running light. One of the novel features of the course was a 2.4-mile tunnel where it would be pitch black, requiring the use of a light. I had purchased one on Friday and was looking forward to using it. The tunnel sounded very cool.

There were only about a hundred racers, and the start was a low-key affair. The weather was cool—still in the 50s. The first part was a pleasant 5-mile out and back that gave us a taste of the scenic views that the website had boasted about. A few miles after the out and back, we reached the tunnel. It really was pitch black. I switched on my light and tried to soak up the experience. My breath condensed as I exhaled, creating a constant cloud in front of my face as I ran, enhancing the surrealness of the experience. After I had been progressing in the tunnel for a while, I noticed a light in the distance. There was, I assumed, some kind of illuminated aid station at the midpoint. It got bigger and bigger until finally I realized it was simply the sun coming in through the opening at the end. I will never hear the expression, "the light at the end of the tunnel," again without thinking of this race.

Soon after leaving the tunnel, the downhill portion of the course began. With the sun shining and the course descending steadily, the temperatures began to move up. It wasn't a problem for me for the first 13 miles or so. I had been targeting an average pace of 10:30-10:40 and held it for most of the first half. After the halfway point, with the temperature climbing to levels that I could no longer ignore, I began to slow, watching as my average pace moved steadily up from 10:40. My other preoccupation, in addition to the building heat of the day, was my left foot. The foot stayed calm through the first eight miles. After that, the discomfort increased, but it never became severely painful and (at least it seemed to me) did not alter my stride or cause any slowing.

With my plantar concerns fading, the heat remained the big story of the day. By mile 16, it had gotten really hot, and my pace was continuing to slow. By mile 22, I knew that a sub-4:50 finish was out of the question. A few miles later, I realized that I had slowed down so much that even a sub-5:00 finish was no longer a certainty. I really wanted to at least salvage that. When I had run Comrades in 2018, a 5-hour marathon was the qualifying standard. Race organizers lowered it to 4:50 in 2019, but to my mind, there would be at least some solace in breaking five hours. As I crossed, I stopped my Garmin - 4:59:59. It was sub-5:00, but the farthest thing from a confidence-building experience imaginable. The only bright spot was that the foot had not been a major problem. At least, I thought, that dragon had been slayed.

Lindsey and I texted about the race afterward. He was pleased that the foot had held up and agreed that the heat was responsible for the dramatic slowing over the last few miles. He remained, as always, brimming with confidence that we could get it done.

CHAPTER 35

San Francisco

My final remaining hurdle before Comrades was the 50K long run, ideally completed five weeks before race day. In 2018, I had done my Comrades long run by tacking 4.8 miles onto the Providence Marathon. With no suitable 50Ks on the calendar, I realized that I would again have to construct my own. Fortunately, the optimal race day for me also happened to be the date of the San Francisco Marathon. It was a big city marathon, on a loop course with great scenery and historically mild temperatures, and it looked like it would be a fun one.

I planned on doing the extra miles before the race, despite its 5:30 a.m. start time. I left my hotel at 4:20, ran a mile to the start, and then headed out for a 3.8 mile out and back. I finished the extra miles right on schedule, hit a porta potty, and went over to the race start. While waiting, I listened to the race announcer, working to get the crowd of sleepy runners excited for the long hours of running ahead. I thought I had heard it all before, but then she said something that was so original and funny that I pulled my phone out and typed it into my Notes app: "If your training went well, we hope you have a great race. If your training did not go according to plan, we hope you have a miraculous day today." Then, a few minutes later, we were off.

The first few miles were nicely flat along the water, a touristy part of the city that I had walked a few years earlier when I had been in San Francisco for a conference. The temperature was in the 50s, and I kept on the throwaway gloves and sleeves that I had purchased for the beginning of the race. As I continued, with more than 20 miles of running still ahead of me, I was reminded how emotionally challenging this part of a marathon can be. In some ways, I always find the early parts of long races the hardest: there is no pain or discomfort, yet there is so much time and work ahead that it can be daunting. I had to push back the question that always begged to be asked at this stage, "Why do I keep putting myself through this?"

As I worked through my early-in-the-race negativity, I decided to try a new tack. For years, as I approached another birthday, particularly milestone ones like my 40th and my 50th, there would inevitably be some sadness over the fact that I was getting older. My fallback, as another birthday approached, was a line that my mother always used to use, "It beats the alternative." A few months before San Francisco, while driving, I pondered my upcoming 60th birthday. At first, my mind went to my mother's expression. I decided though that it was a negative way of thinking about advancing age: "Yeah, it sucks, but it could be worse; I could be dead."

I needed a more positive way of looking at it, and then it came to me. My proper attitude should be to reflect on how lucky I was to reach this milestone. My second book, *Fighting Back*, had just been published. It told the story of Stan Andrews, a WWII bomber pilot and an extraordinarily talented artist and writer who had gone to Israel in 1948 to participate in that country's war of independence. Stan had been killed on a combat mission shortly after turning 25. What would he have given, I thought, to have lived these additional 35 years? Turning 60, I concluded, was a privilege that was not given to everyone, and I should be grateful to receive it. As I worked through those early miles, I decided to try a version of this positive thinking. I tried to counter the "why am I putting myself through this" thoughts with "isn't it amazing that I have a body that allows me to do this at 60?" If nothing else, it kept my mind occupied until the funk had passed.

I was excited about the next phase of the race. We were to climb from the waterfront up to the Golden Gate Bridge and then run across to Marin, where we would have a several mile loop before coming back across and continuing the main route through the city. One of the reasons why I chose San Francisco was the topography of the course. With Comrades getting closer, I was getting anxious about the fact that almost all my training had been on the pancake flat terrain of south Florida. The hilly sections of the San Francisco Marathon would expose me to climbing and descending— in a race setting—just a few months before going back to South Africa.

Lindsey had given me two strategies to try for the uphills: 1-minute running/1-minute walking and 90-seconds running/1-minute walking. I played with both as I climbed toward the bridge, and each seemed to work fine. Running on the bridge was a delight. It was scenic, breezy, and invigorating. After leaving the bridge and entering Marin, we continued along a straight and flat section for a while and then began to descend along a road that was both sharply downhill and banked to the right. After a few minutes of this, my left foot really began to hurt. I kept searching for a flatter part of the road, but there was no escaping the slant and no stopping the discomfort. It wasn't a sharp pain that caused me to want to stop, but it was uncomfortable—and I still had about 17 miles of running ahead of me. It would, I realized, be a long day. Hearkening back to my rumination from earlier in the race, at that moment I understood that while I needed to be grateful that I had a 60-year-old body that was going to allow me to run 31 miles, at least on this day it would be with a lot of pain.

A few years earlier, I saw a quote from ultra-runner Ann Trason: "It hurts up to a point, and then it doesn't get any worse." I always reminded myself of this over the period of a long event as soreness and discomfort settled in. It protected against catastrophizing: to assume that if it hurts this much at mile 13, imagine how awful it will be at mile 20 or 25. Her observation really did hold true in my experience. The exception was the acute event, whether muscle spasms from dehydration as I had experienced at Steamtown or the dramatic recurrence of a debilitating injury. Still, as long as my foot pain stayed within the confines of the Trason definition, I knew I could pound out the miles, however ugly it might be.

The course meandered around Marin, through parks and across a small nature preserve until we found ourselves approaching the bridge for the return to San Francisco. The miles kept ticking by, across Golden Gate Park and then the famous neighborhood of Haight Ashbury.

The foot pain remained more or less constant. While it didn't force me to adjust my stride, it destroyed my speed. Lindsey had wanted me to target an average pace of 12:30 minutes per mile, but I couldn't hold it. I went back and forth over whether continuing the race was the right decision. Having already missed so many long runs in the months since my plantar struggles had begun, I was convinced that pulling out of this race would put a definite end to my Comrades quest. I resolved to finish the run as long as the foot didn't completely erupt in pain and hobble me, so that I could at least lock in the endurance benefit. I promised myself that I would rest and get serious about rehab as soon as I got back home.

After mile 24, we reached the water and turned toward the finish. I crossed, got my medal and some post-race refreshments, and started the walk back to my hotel. My foot had had it with me; the return seemed to take forever. I had mixed feelings as I limped through the city streets, the finisher's medal around my neck. It was always nice to complete a marathon, especially having tacked on the additional miles, but I knew the race had not been a success.

I thought I had beaten plantar but clearly had not. I now only had five weeks to rest, recover, rehab, and somehow pull it all together for Comrades.

CHAPTER 36

The Why

I was able to get a physical therapist appointment for the day after my return from San Francisco. The PT identified weakness in my hip as the likely cause of an imbalance that had led to the plantar and took me through a series of exercises to try to address it. She also suggested dry needling, and I enthusiastically agreed.

As I went through the exercises, I mentally kicked myself for not having thought to go for physical therapy months earlier. The hip weakness was something that my old PT Rachel Miller had identified years before, and I realized it must be a fundamental issue with me that needed regular attention. In the lead up to Comrades in 2018, I had been very diligent about going to Rachel to try to head off an injury, an increasingly common practice among serious athletes known as "prehab." This time the focus and preparation had not been there, and now I only had about five weeks to play catch-up while also squeezing in potentially two weeks of unscheduled rest to recover from San Francisco. It was not a recipe for success.

Over the next month, I came in twice a week for standard physical therapy sessions and also received three intensely painful dry-needling treatments. It seemed to be helping, but I could still sense that the foot was not completely normal. Nine days after San Francisco, I tentatively resumed running, and a week after that I completed a 3-hour long run with no real pain—a success but, with only three weeks until race day, it was hard to get too excited about it. That would have to be my last long run before Comrades, and I still wasn't convinced that the foot would hold up under race conditions.

Having done everything I felt that I could to deal with the plantar, I also began to focus on other pre-race tasks that I had been neglecting. One of these was to watch a Comrades training webinar, given by Lindsey as the official coach, on race day strategy. I had watched a previous version of it in 2018, but I needed to refresh my memory of the course profile and the pacing decisions that I would need to make for particularly challenging climbs or descents.

In the webinar, Lindsey talked about the need to remember your "why." He explained that it would be critical as you persevered in the face of the hours of pain and discomfort that you were going to experience on race day. It was the kind of thing that I had heard many times before, and yet it occurred to me that I had never stopped to really ponder what my personal "why" was. As I now thought about it, I realized that there were several layers to it for me. The superficial "why" was that the Comrades race, from the first time I read about it, spoke to me in a powerful way. Perhaps it is because of its origin story—as a living memorial to soldiers who died in WWI, with the goal of "celebrat[ing] mankind's spirit over adversity" (Comrades Marathon, 2022). As someone who has long been drawn to military history, a focus of my two prior books, I found that inspiring.

Comrades did something else for me. I have always liked the idea of chasing after interesting things that are challenging and that take time, like completing my first year of law school in a new language, obtaining a master's degree in international law at night while working full-time as a lawyer (with the added goal, after seeing my first semester's grades, of finishing first in the class), writing my first two books, taking two full semesters of chemistry and biology classes to qualify for the patent bar exam, and getting a second master's degree after joining the start-up. Then, when endurance sports became a passion for me, it was the chase after that first marathon, the first half-Ironman, and ultimately that first full Ironman. Each goal, in different ways, required long periods of focused effort. And it was the extended effort that made the ultimate accomplishments particularly meaningful and, in their own way, life-altering.

In 2017 and 2018, as I got ready for my first Comrades, it had all been somewhat straightforward. I qualified, did the training precisely as laid out in the plan, gave what I regarded as my best effort, and came close. I had assumed that, at age 56, this was my one shot. I was always a marginal candidate to finish the race anyway and it would only get harder as I got older. But, reading stories by endurance athletes I admired, for example, David Goggins' two failed attempts at breaking the world record for pull-ups before finally succeeding on this third try—the idea of dusting myself off and trying again had its own appeal. Sometimes, for the things that really matter, we have to be prepared to try, fail, and then get back up and try again.

And what of all those injuries? I had long ago accepted them as part of the endurance sports lifestyle, as a cost of doing business. Statistically, most runners will deal with injury at some point. Study conclusions vary, but between 30% and 75% of runners can expect to get injured each year. But that can be, perversely, part of the attraction. As ultra-runner and documentary film maker Billy Yang (2018) expressed it in one of his films: "When it's your time is the goal to leave a well-preserved body? Or do you really want to use it? A body with stories that says you've pushed it, and at times suffered, and you sought its potential." Or, as put with perhaps less delicateness by Hunter S. Thompson (1998), "Life should not be a journey to the grave with the intention of arriving safely in a pretty and well preserved body but rather to skid in broadside in a cloud of smoke, thoroughly used up, totally worn out, and loudly proclaiming 'Wow! What a Ride!'"

As I got ready for my second attempt at Comrades, I realized that I had looked at big, new challenges, whether a marathon, Olympic distance triathlon, a 50K or Comrades, as something at which I would always succeed if I just did the work. Failing, figuring out why, and then trying again was, of course, its own essential life lesson. If I were serious about pursuing sports as a metaphor for life, I needed to incorporate return after failure as well. Fittingly, the motto for 2022 Comrades was "The Return"—Sishay'ibuya—

chosen to celebrate the resumption of Comrades after two years of Covid cancellations.

My "why" had another layer as well. I have always been drawn to the aspirational, the audacious. I admire people who take on great challenges, who live daring lives. Often, when confronted with a difficult situation, I try to think of myself as a character in a movie and imagine how someone sitting in the theater might react upon watching me. Would he/she be impressed and inspired by what they saw on the big screen, or disappointed? To me, taking on Comrades was a manifestation of my desire to be daring, to live a big life, one that would impress that imagined theatergoer. Perhaps more to the point, I wanted to live a life that would impress and inspire *me,* whether 17-year-old me, who would be amazed to learn what was still in store as I got so much older (and, let's face it, to a 17-year-old, 60 is *old*) or end-of-life-me, looking back on a life lived greatly, with few regrets.

I have always bristled at the refrain about how no one, on their death bed, regrets not having spent more time in the office. Putting to one side what people think in the emotional turmoil that accompanies literally the last minutes of life and what the actual value of that supposed insight might be, I suspect that many people, in the decades of life that follow what should have been their personal and professional peak years, look back with longing and regret on chances not taken, opportunities missed because of risks avoided, and potential not realized. I believe that what we most regret in life are the things we don't try.

As I looked back at my life from the vantage point of 60, I had my share of regrets and disappointments, to be sure. But I also looked at my kids, at my books, at my professional accomplishments, at my academic successes, and at my athletic feats. There was much that made me feel that I had realized at least a significant part of my potential. I was proud that I had challenged myself and wanted to keep doing that.

So, that was my "why," I decided. Running Comrades a second time would be me living my best life, my daring life, my life of pursuing greatness. It would be about overcoming adversity, of being unafraid, of being willing to fail, of trying again after failing, and of accepting pain and sacrifice in the pursuit of a lofty goal. And it would be about me chasing my potential, of trying to become a me that I will look back on with pride rather than sadness and regret.

CHAPTER 37

The Return

I traveled back to South Africa, arriving a few days before the race. I was well into the taper and would have no idea about the condition of my foot or the consequences of all the missed workouts until the race was underway. All I could do was wait and worry.

On the Thursday before the big day, with the Expo set to open, I arranged to have coffee with Lindsey. It would be my first opportunity to meet him in person. He was as compelling in real life as in his Podcast and in our Skype sessions: kind, thoughtful, positive, and a font of running insights. We talked a bit about Lindsey's father, an extraordinary runner who had once completed Comrades in less than six hours, finishing 6th overall in the race, and whose personal best marathon was an extraordinary 2 hours 20 minutes. He was in his 70s now but, with Lindsey's help, had restructured his training and in recent years had surprised himself with some great times. He would be running the Boston marathon with Lindsey in the spring and was even toying with the idea of taking on Comrades again. One of the keys to his late success, Lindsey told me, was the way he had taken to strength training, the same strength training that I was supposed to have been doing for the last half year. While I had done resistance work for my legs twice a week, I stayed with the leg curl and leg extension machines that I had been using for years rather than the running-specific, body weight exercises that Lindsey had recommended. As I heard Lindsey talk with pride about what his father was accomplishing, I chided myself for not having taken his specific leg routine more seriously. It was too late now.

Lindsey drove me to the Expo, where he headed off to prepare for a talk that he would be giving. I went to the foreign runners' desk to pick up my race bibs (two of them: one for the front and one for the back, another unique Comrades tradition). After that, I wandered around the main exhibition area looking for souvenirs, picking up some keychains and a Comrades coffee table book.

As I had dissected my near-miss in 2018, I identified several areas in which I had lost valuable minutes on race day. A significant one and, it turned out, a surprisingly easy one to address, had to do with my starting corral. The slowest qualifiers were placed in H Batch and, in 2018, that had cost me nearly 11 minutes, which alone may have been the difference between success and failure. Turning in a faster qualifying time and moving to a better corral was out of the question. Just moving up to G would have required me to lower my marathon PR to below 4:35. However, after the race, I discovered that by making a several hundred-dollar contribution to one of the approved race charities, I would be in C batch, much closer to the start line. I signed up with a childhood cancer charity called the Super Moos, excited that this one fix alone would more than erase my margin of failure from last time. Wandering around the Expo, I saw their table and went over to introduce myself and pick up a themed t-shirt.

I then went to look for some gels—Vanilla Bean to be precise—but I was not buying them for myself. For my first Comrades, I had persuaded my little brother Josh to meet me in South Africa for the experience. I had been a 19-year-old college sophomore when Josh was born but, despite the age gap, we had always been close. He had enjoyed his time in South Africa in 2018 and had been bitten by the bug. When I had been gearing up to try again in 2020, Josh had toyed with the idea of taking up running and trying it with me, but a hip injury would have prevented that even if Covid hadn't intervened. With 2022 set to happen, Josh had a proposal for me. If he trained and qualified and then the two of us started the race together, I would have to go to the Burning Man festival with him in the Nevada desert the following year. Josh was a tremendous athlete and a coach who still played baseball and soccer at a high level but had essentially no experience with distance running. So, even though Burning Man was not exactly on my list of new things to try, it seemed like a safe deal to make.

More than a half year before the close of the qualifying window, after some initial promising training, Josh had gone to South America for an extended travel adventure. As he moved from country to country, he did his best to keep up with his training, but I could tell that it lacked consistency.

He also injured his calf, which further interfered with things. Increasingly, it seemed to me and with some amount of relief, there would be no Burning Man in my future.

To qualify, Josh had picked out a course in Montana with even more downhill than the one I had found in Seattle. The problem with Josh's race was that it was literally the day before the qualifying window closed. If there was any glitch on race day, that would be the end of it. And given that he had never even run a half marathon before, I worried that the lack of formal race experience could result in him either going out too slowly and being unable to make up time later in the race, or, more likely, going out too quickly and then blowing up after mile 20. I tried to talk him into coming to Seattle with me so that we could run together in controlled conditions, but he discussed it with Lindsey, who was also coaching Josh, and they both felt that Josh's calf needed more recovery time.

On the day of the Montana race, I waited for him to call, intensely interested in how it had gone. I hoped that he would qualify but, at the same time, had to admit to myself that a miss would at least get me off the hook from going to Burning Man. He called shortly after finishing. He had run an excellent race and had broken 4:30. With that, Comrades and Burning Man were on. Josh planned to join me in South Africa a few days after I arrived, and he had asked me to pick up the Vanilla Bean gels for him.

Another mistake in my first race had been to spend the night in Durban, which had required a middle-of-the-night bus ride to Pietermaritzburg. To be able to sleep closer to the race start, I had taken a suggestion from Lindsey and signed up for a Comrades race support package with Markus van Niekerk. Markus had previously been part of Lindsey's coaching team before going on to form Race Tours, which specialized in organizing the logistics for destination races like Comrades. Markus had organized a hotel room near Pietermaritzburg for the night before the race, and he would drive us to the start on race morning, all of which would get me several hours of extra sleep. In the days that I spent in South Africa waiting for Josh to arrive, I spent a lot of time with Markus and with Trevor and Tash, a couple from England who were also on the tour. This would be Trevor's first try at Comrades.

On the Friday morning before the race, my plan (and Trevor's) called for a 20-minute shakeout run. Markus took us down to the waterfront area in Durban to do it and planned on running with us. When he removed a sweatshirt before we got started, I noticed a tattoo of a mountain on the inside of his left upper arm. I asked if it was any particular one. No, he told me, it was symbolic of something he had once heard: "If you want to enjoy the view, you need to climb the mountain."

Markus had arranged a dinner for that night, to be attended by all the runners on his tour, with Lindsey as the special guest to talk about race strategy. I was looking forward to that. By now, I had heard Lindsey give versions of the same talk several times, but each time I learned something new about the course. It was, for me, such a complicated puzzle that I hoped through repetition, at least some of the main watchouts would sink in and help me on race day.

Josh would not be there for the talk. His travel had gone completely haywire, beginning with a delayed flight that cost him his connection in Istanbul. After being forced to spend the night in Turkey, he managed to get a flight to Tanzania early the next morning and then one to Johannesburg, but he could not find a flight for the more than 300-mile trip from Johannesburg to Durban. Lindsey saved the day, arranging for a friend who was already planning to drive in for the race to pick up Josh from the airport. Josh arrived late Friday night, over 24 hours later than he had planned, exhausted from the extended travel and hours of missed sleep. His bag had not arrived with him. It appeared to have never left Tanzania, and he was missing some gear, including the underwear that he liked to wear under his running shorts. It was not, I thought, a hopeful sign for how he might do on race day. Still, his spirits were high, and he was excited to finally be in Durban.

The next morning, Josh went to the Expo to pick up his race number and to hand in his drop bags. In the afternoon, Markus loaded us into a van for the trip to the hotel outside of Pietermaritzburg, where we would be staying for the night before the race. On the way, we stopped at a mall so that Josh could try to find replacement dry-fit underwear, but the best he could do was something from a local brand that he could only hope would be comfortable for the long hours of running the next day. They say that you should never try anything new on race day—and most of all that you should never *wear* anything you haven't first tried out in training—but desperate times call for desperate measures.

The underwear search was the latest in a long line of silent eye-rolling moments for me. I couldn't help but be a little disdainful about the cavalier way that Josh had been approaching the whole venture. Though he was an extraordinary athlete, his run training had been spotty. His extended travel in South America during what should have been his peak training months had cost him numerous long runs and had prevented him from accumulating any meaningful race experience. When I ran Comrades in 2018, I had run four races of at least 26.2 miles in the prior eight months, including three in the last 90 days before the race. In Josh's case, after months of inconsistent training that had been interrupted by a calf injury, he had run only a single marathon and that on an extreme downhill course literally the day before the qualifying window closed. I was delighted to have him with me and excited about our upcoming shared adventure, but I just couldn't decide who was going to be helping whom once the race began the next morning. And why the fuck hadn't he put a pair of running underwear in his carry-on just in case his checked bag didn't make it?

But Josh's enthusiasm and honest joy about what we were about to do were irresistible. While I spent those last days consumed with worry, he was having a ball, seemingly without a care in the world. He had shirts printed for the two of us to wear during the race, which, to my chagrin, he *did* think to put in his carry-on. His had a number "7" on the front, signifying that he was the 7th child in the family, while mine had a number "3" for my place in the birth order. On the back it said:

JEFF WEISS –
YOU ARE AWESOME
WITH AN IRON BODY
BUT STILL A FOOL
WHO RUNS 90 KM
THE WEISS BOYS!
FINISH BY 11:59
I LOVE YOU
GO MAN GO

With Josh scheduled to arrive on Thursday, I had told him that I would wear the shirt for my practice run on Friday, and, if it felt fine, I would wear it for the race. I am nothing if not conventional when it comes to the rule of "nothing new on race day." But Josh's flight delay had deprived me of the ability to try the shirt Friday morning, and now I had a decision to make. At first, I resolved to wear it anyway. He was just so enthusiastic, and I hated the idea of disappointing him. But after trying it on and sensing that it was a little tight and the material not particularly comfortable, I rebelled. I told him, apologetically, that I wouldn't wear it. He was disappointed but remained irrepressibly upbeat.

We checked into our new hotel around 4:00 and had a few hours to unwind before dinner. Now that I was in the room that I would be waking up in on race morning, I began to lay out all my clothes and gear for the race. As recommended by Lindsey, I had prepared a formal checklist, and I physically crossed off each item as I laid it out. Everything was there. I met Josh, Trevor, and Markus for dinner. The hotel was magnificent. It had the feel of a luxury mountain resort, but I was having trouble relaxing. The other three were all in high spirits, but I could only focus on wolfing down my food and getting back to my room to try to rectify one of my biggest mistakes from 2018, which had been the failure to get any meaningful sleep the night before the race.

I turned off the lights by 9:45, as planned. In 2018, I had wrestled with whether to take a Benadryl to help fall asleep and ultimately had not, only to later regret that decision. This was another opportunity to correct a prior mistake. But, even with the Benadryl, I found myself wide awake, tossing and turning as the minutes ticked by. I was avoiding looking at my watch so as not to add to my anxiety but finally checked it and saw that it was past 11. My alarm was set for 3:20 a.m., We needed to be at the van by 3:40, and my sleep window was closing. I took a second half of a Benadryl. That did it. A short while later, I finally fell asleep and stayed that way until my alarm woke me at 3:20. It hadn't been perfect, but it was a huge improvement over 2018.

I quickly got organized and was the first one out to the van. Josh and Trevor arrived a few minutes later. As we waited for the rest of our group, I chatted with Trevor. He and his wife had been tremendous companions for the last several days. They had been taken with the idea of Josh and I tackling the race as brothers, particularly given the age gap. They were originally from South Africa and had moved to England a few years earlier. Trevor was in his 40s—young compared to me—and was also big to be a runner, a few inches over six feet and stocky. He had only been running for a few years and would be starting in H batch, but had that quiet confidence that seemed to be a South African trademark. We hugged before we boarded. "I would bet anything that you will finish," I told him.

There was a fair amount of traffic as we got closer to the city, and it wasn't until 4:45 that we pulled into a gas station that looked to be about a half mile down the street from where the starting corrals were located. Markus and all the others in the van were excited, but I was stressed. We weren't at our corral yet, and I had read that at 5 a.m. they closed the entrances to the corrals, and you had to go to the back, behind H batch. As I looked up the street, I realized that we still had a decent walk ahead of us, with potentially only 15 minutes left to get into position. If we missed it, that would be the end of C and perhaps the ten or more minutes of time savings that it represented.

I had to hustle Josh away from the van, where he and everyone else were lingering, unconcerned about the time. We started walking toward the start. When we reached the back of the corrals, we had to move onto a crowded sidewalk that was in a serious state of disrepair. The minutes were ticking by: 4:52, 4:53, …. I kept moving forward through a thick crowd, nearly tripping several times on the broken-up sidewalk. At each succeeding corral entry, there was a choke point as runners queued up to enter. We finally reached the entrance to C, where Josh and I would be starting together, at precisely 4:59. We entered, to my immense relief, and headed to the right side of the corral. With the race about to start, we needed to strip off our throwaway sweatpants and sweatshirts. I would keep on my gloves and sleeves and had purchased a set for Josh as well. Amidst our frenzied movements, Josh somehow managed to lose one of his gloves, and I had to suppress another eye roll.

The C corral placement was even better than I had imagined, and we seemed to be no more than 50 yards from the archway that stretched over the official start line. In 2018 it had not even been visible to me from where I had been standing. At 5:15, the barriers that separated the corrals were dropped, and we all moved forward, even closer to the start, which now seemed to be literally a stone's throw away. This was also the signal for the Comrades rituals to begin. First, the national anthem, with which Josh and I could do very little other than the last line of the English language portion ("South Africa our land!"). It was followed by *Shosholoza*, which I had been practicing and now actually knew, and I sang along with gusto. That was followed by *Chariots of Fire*. After a lengthy pause, there was Max Trimborn's legendary rooster crow. And then, with a cannon shot, the race was officially started, and we were moving.

CHAPTER 38

Passing the Baton

We crossed under the arch in just over a minute, more than 9:40 faster than in 2018. Combined with the extra sleep compared to 2018, as the race started I had already corrected two major mistakes from my first attempt. It was still dark as we moved downhill through Pietermaritzburg, which did not take long at all, precisely as I remembered. Polly Shorts, the first of the big five hills, came almost immediately after we left town and we descended, running comfortably. As we climbed back up, with the sun rising and with it the temperature, I ditched my outer shirt and sleeves and, not long after that, the gloves as well.

We were slightly below, by a second or two, the 7:46 kilometers per minute target pace that Lindsey had set for us for the day—or, more accurately, between 7:46 (for an 11:45 finish) and 7:56 (for a 12:00 finish). He had also given us a chart, which we had laminated, that had individual pace targets for each 10K segment, given the changes in topography that we would be encountering. We cleared the 80K sign a few minutes ahead of schedule, and I hit the lap function on my Garmin to start the next 10K, which was supposed to be a little slower. I was looking forward to the 75KM sign and the first checkpoint. We hit it in good form—about 38 minutes before the cut-off time, again a huge improvement over 2018 and another confidence builder. The rest of the second 10K included a tough stretch from 16K to 20K that Lindsey had warned about in his Friday night talk. We modified our run/walk, but it wasn't that bad. We finished the second 10K, again a shade ahead of schedule, and I started the third lap.

Josh was in great spirits, talking the whole way. I talked too for most of the first 10K and then began to ration my responses and then finally told him that I would only speak on walk breaks. I was worried that talking while running might cost me valuable energy. I was taking in gels at about 40-minute intervals, drinking Gatorade, and also grabbing water. My system felt better than in 2018, when I just seemed to have no appetite right from the beginning. I noticed that the crowds were thicker than I remembered, perhaps because I was so much farther forward in the race pack than I had been the last time. I was finally experiencing some of that crowd magic that so many Comrades runners had talked about.

My foot was holding up well but, as we progressed through the third 10K, I could sense that I was slowing. I was having trouble keeping the pace close to the 7:46 KPM average, and the first doubts started to creep in. We finished the third 10K, missing the time for that segment but still ahead of schedule overall. It was getting warmer, and I decided to start taking salt tablets to get ahead of the muscle spasms from 2018. I was excited to get to the 60K sign and the first bag drop. We got there, grabbed our stuff, and kept moving. I took one bite from a peanut butter and jelly sandwich that I had prepared but was otherwise sticking with gels. Josh was taking in a lot more calories than I was, eating and drinking everything in sight.

I kept wondering about the left foot, but it stayed as it had been on my most recent training runs—slightly off but no pain. My left knee, however, did start to bother me for whatever reason. It had never hurt in training, and I hoped that it would just resolve itself. (My right knee, the one with the osteoarthritis diagnosis, remained pain-free.)

Josh told me that he was sensing a hot spot on one of his toes and wanted to find tape at an aid station that he could apply. I thought that was nuts—he would surely lose a lot of time—but he was determined. We agreed that I would continue along the left side of the road and that way, when he finished and caught up, he would know where to find me. Over the next few hours we did the same drill a few more times while he headed off to pee, find salt, or grab some food. I worried that he would wear himself out with these "interval" sessions of acceleration to catch back up to me. He was totally confident, assuring me that to catch up he was simply running his normal pace and that he felt great. I was convinced that he just didn't know what was in store, that having run only a single marathon he did not understand the toll that a long race takes on the body. But I had to be careful. I did not want to dent his confidence, which I admired.

As the sun came out. it warmed up and then began to get hot, beyond what I had expected from the forecasts. We saw two runners at the side of the road being attended by medics, likely the victims of heat stroke. I was anxious to get to Drummond/half-way and, more specifically, through the climb out to Alveston where the "downhill" part of the down run really begins. We passed Arthur's seat. This time I just tipped my cap, but Josh ran over and did the whole thing. I was still slowing. I tried to look around more and take in the views, hoping it might distract me from the growing distress about how my race was going. The surrounding lush hills were not, however, enough to make me forget my situation. I was slowing down and my Comrades dream was slipping away. I heard a 12-hour "bus" coming up behind me and instinctively moved farther to the left so that it could pass. The driver, a woman, called out in a gentle voice, reading my name off the bib on my back, "It's okay, Jeffrey. We are all in this together. We are all soldiers." I was surprised and moved by her words, but the passing of her bus confirmed that I was in deep trouble.

Coming out of Drummond was challenging. The uphills were steep, and my walk breaks were getting longer. Josh kept asking if I could walk faster, if I could run a bit in places where I was walking, and, when I could run, if I could do that faster. I was saying no to pretty much all his suggestions, feeling very depleted. At one point, during a walk break, he put a hand on the small of my back and gave me a little bit of a push as we walked together. A short while later he told me to put my arm around his shoulder, and

I reluctantly agreed, realizing that the wheels were really coming off.

We were now steadily losing minutes off our target according to Lindsey's more conservative plan. I was increasingly realizing that it was not to be. I just could not imagine enough of a second wind that would rescue me. I was becoming convinced that all the missed workouts because of the plantar had just left me way too undertrained. On top of that, the left knee pain was not going away. It was killing my pace and making it hard to start back up after walk breaks.

I reminded Josh that he should go ahead the moment it became clear that his ability to finish was in jeopardy, something we had discussed in the lead-up to the race. He rebuffed me, assuring me that he was committed to staying and that we would both make it. He was confident that if it really came to separating at some point, he could easily make up the lost time. We went back and forth this way for a few kilometers. At one point, I tried a different tack. "You're an athlete and a coach. When you can tell that I'm done, you should tell me, and then you should go on." That also did not work.

Bailer buses were passing by, and I felt sorry for the people on them. At one point, I saw someone with a yellow number (9 finishes, going for green) climb on. The heat clearly was a factor, especially for the locals who had been training during the South African winter. At one point, some emergency vehicles and an ambulance passed by quickly, sirens blaring. We found out later that it was taking a runner who had collapsed to the hospital, where he was pronounced dead. A second runner also died during the race.

I just couldn't find that next gear. I couldn't pick up the pace on the runs or the walks, and I realized that I was risking Josh's race for no good reason. We had just passed the 39 km sign, and I realized that it was now or never. I turned to Josh and said, "I'm not going to make it. You need to go on by yourself. If you don't, I am going to climb on the next bailer bus." He was horrified. He asked me not to, again arguing that I could finish. I told him that if he would go on right now, I would stay in the race until the next cut-off at 33 km. I told him that if he finished, it would have all been worthwhile but that if he didn't, it really would not have been. He finally agreed. We hugged, and he shouted, "I love this man," and headed out.

I felt a surge of relief as he moved away, the guilt over holding him back lifting. I did not know what to make of his chances. He was nearly 20 years younger, a terrific athlete, and supremely confident, but I just didn't know how he would hold up to the mounting kilometers, given his limited racing experience. I tried to run steadily for the next kilometer, during a nice long downhill stretch, to see if perhaps there was another gear after all. As I ran, I kept looking at the screen on my Garmin that showed my average pace for the whole distance to that point. It was at 8:18 kilometers per minute and then, after a few minutes, went up to 8:19. That decided it for me. My race was done.

This then became my Comrades: keeping my promise to Josh and toughing it out to 33 km even though I had no chance to finish. I walked almost the whole distance, both from a lack of energy but also out of a desire to avoid truly hurting the left knee or possibly bringing on heat stroke. Slowly, agonizingly slowly, the kilometers ticked down as I continued along a course that was rapidly emptying of both runners and spectators. I felt virtuous as I walked, though. I was pleased that I was keeping my end of the bargain and happy that I had released Josh in sufficient time for him to have a shot at making it to the finish.

As the walking minutes mounted, I could see that I would truly miss the 33 km cut-off. When I finally reached it, the other stragglers and I were directed to a bus. As I took a seat, I noticed that the other runners all seemed lighthearted, unlike what I had experienced in 2018 when we had all gotten cut so late in the race. In many ways, missing by a lot is emotionally easier than missing by a little, and we had all missed by a lot.

After arriving at the stadium, I found the international runners' entrance. My legs had completely stiffened, and walking was challenging and painful. But unlike in 2018 when I had run 51 miles, this time, having only gone a little over 35, I did not feel that I had earned the pain. I got a beer and some cake, my first breaking of nutrition discipline in seven weeks. I found a chair and texted Markus and Tash. They were in a different part of the stadium, and I took my time. There were still two and a half hours until the finish.

Josh had told me at one point that he had put his phone in airplane mode to conserve battery life, which meant he could not be live tracked from the app. I was going to have to wait until he hit the timing mats at each cut-off to be able to find out if he had in fact been making up time. I kept staring at my phone, and when he hit 33 km, the app updated to show an 8:24 average pace for that section and a projected 12:19 finish, which of course meant that he would not make it to the stadium. I couldn't tell how much of this was still a legacy of my slowing him down during the first part of the run. The next cut-off would tell the tale.

When he passed the 21 km cut-off, it all changed. His pace for that section dropped to 6:50, and his projected finish time to 11:59:13. He really was making up the lost time, but could he hold it? I would have another hour or so to wait until he reached the 9 km cut-off at Sherwood, where my race had ended in 2018. He hit that one, and his pace was 7:24 for the segment. His projected finish was just a shade over 11:52. He still had to hang on, but, incredibly, it seemed like he would actually do it.

By now, I had found Tash, and we grabbed seats near the finish line. She was solicitous about my pain and about my not having made it. I wasn't sure she believed me, but I assured her that a Josh finish would vindicate the entire day for me. Trevor was still out there as well, less than a minute ahead of Josh, which was incredibly exciting. Tash showed me a "map" function on the app which displayed an icon of your runner on the course. Josh must have turned off airplane mode because it had him progressing, close behind Trevor, still with a projected 11:52 finish. When it seemed clear that Josh must be entering the stadium, I searched but could not find him. Tash couldn't find Trevor either. We doubled-checked the app, which said they had each finished, and we were both ecstatic.

Josh later told me that when he was about 90 minutes from the finish, still feeling good, he caught up with one of the 12-hour busses, the one led by the woman who had spoken so kindly to me during the race. Rather than pass it, he decided to join the group, confident that she would get them across. That was what threw me. The bus had finished right before I expected that he would, and it had not occurred to me that he had been on it, in the sea of runners crossing as a group.

I was reunited with Josh within a few minutes, and we shared a big hug. He was beaming, a huge smile on his face, wearing his finisher's medal. I finally got to examine one up close. It was light and tiny, perhaps no more than a quarter the size of a typical marathon finisher's medal for a U. S. race—and yet there was an unmistakable mystique to it. Small or not, I would have loved to have earned one myself. But truly, seeing how thrilled Josh was and still in awe over how magnificently he handled the entire day, it was the next best thing.

CHAPTER 39

What Next?

As I lay in bed later that night, I reflected on what the day had meant to me and the lessons that I should draw from it. I was conscious of the fact that it was all still quite raw and that my initial reactions might not ultimately be the correct ones, but I wanted to capture them while the day's events were still so fresh. I was happy for Josh and proud of what he had done. There was no waffling on that, no tinge of jealousy creeping into my thinking. The rest of it was far more complicated.

There were some things I was certain about. My commitment to fitness was unshakeable. I felt that the *Younger Next Year* prescription of six days of fitness per week would always be right for me. I needed to continue to attend to the physical not just for my health but also to retain as much youthful vitality for as long as I reasonably could. The increases that exercise gave me in energy, resilience, grit, and optimism—and, of course, improved health—were directly translatable to every area of my life. I wanted all of that to continue.

But what of extreme endurance racing? That was not part of the *Younger Next Year* formula. I had liked chasing progressively more difficult races because they pushed me, with each new success giving me an increased sense of what I might be able to accomplish in the world, in anything that was important to me. But had I taken it too far? Working out six days a week for at least 45 minutes each time is, I believe, an excellent addition to almost any life. It certainly had been for me. Is it necessary, however, to do 2-3 times that in order to live an Ironman or ultramarathon lifestyle? That amount of training placed enormous demands on my time and, much as I tended to focus on the positives, certainly required sacrifice from others. This was especially true of Orlie, who had to put up with a boyfriend who got up every morning at 5 a.m., struggled to stay awake for a television show or movie, went to bed exhausted by 10 p.m., and needed to take most of every Sunday morning for a long workout.

To compound matters, fitness was not the only thing competing for those precious hours not already claimed by my relationship and a demanding work schedule. Writing was also a passion. It was another area in which I had been able to push myself to do things—write books—that my younger self never would have thought possible and that I believe my end-of-life self will look back on with pride. (My second book had come out three months before Comrades, and I was already at work on my next one.) Writing also gives necessary focus to my reading that is similar to how races shape and direct my training. Writing makes my reading purposeful, organizing it into research for the next big project. Unlike either training or racing, I actually enjoy writing while I am doing it. But it takes time. Several years earlier, I committed myself to writing at least one hour per day, first thing in the morning before working out so as to complete both before the start of the workday, another habit that I had resolved to continue for as long as I am physically and mentally able.

The other issue that I had increasingly struggled with, particularly in my second attempts at Comrades and Ironman, had been the stress. The days leading up to each of those two races had been agonizing, filled with worry about how it might go. Invariably, I would find myself wondering why I continued to put myself through this emotional gauntlet, particularly for something that was supposed to be the "fun" part of my life. Balanced against that was my love of seeking out new challenges and of overcoming the mental limitations that I had unwittingly placed on myself. I always liked the line, usually attributed to Eleanor Roosevelt, "Do one thing every day that scares you." Her actual quote was less pithy but far more thoughtful: "You gain strength, courage and confidence by every experience in which you really stop to look fear in the face. You are able to say to yourself, 'I have lived through this horror. I can take the next thing that comes along.' You must do the thing you think you cannot do" (Roosevelt, 2016). And yet, where does it end?

The next day my oldest son texted me, "[S]o glad you were able to do Comrades! Sorry about the result, but I think for you it's more about the training and overall experience and giving it your all rather than the actual outcome. Still, I know it stings!"

I responded, "Your text . . . captures it all perfectly. It does sting. I'm glad I did it. It was about the training and the experience. Very happy for Josh, etc. Lots of swirling emotions. In the end, I really like the idea of chasing dreams, even stretch ones, knowing there is a chance that I may come up short. And along the way, Comrades led me to Ultras, to Ironman, and made me fitter than I ever thought possible."

Craig, another of my brothers, also texted to ask how I was feeling. In answering him, I talked more expansively about what Josh's finish had meant to me. It was not just the pride I felt as an older brother. It was also the knowledge that he had done something extraordinary and lasting because of something I had put in motion. As I wrote Craig, "Josh's performance is a huge silver lining. At least, I can take comfort in planting the crazy Comrades idea in his head. Lots of folks like me who devote a ton of time to sport try to justify it on the ground that they are inspiring others in their lives to reach higher. I have actually never been a huge fan of that. I think it's a way for those of us who take so much time away from the others in our lives to chase after our own dreams to justify our actions. At the end of the day, there is a lot of selfishness involved in chasing things like Ironman and Comrades. But here it actually happened, and he now has something he will cherish for the rest of his life."

The next day I got out of bed feeling uncomfortably good, so much better than I had in 2018. I was spent but not shattered. Josh, on the other hand, was feeling the effects of the race and his extraordinary effort not just to cover the distance but also to make up minutes of lost time during the last 38 kilometers. In the afternoon, we headed over to the same post-race party I had attended in 2018, with Bruce Fordyce again as the master of ceremonies. I had fantasized for the last few years about coming back to the party, this time with a medal around my neck and an inspiring comeback story to tell. I had the next best thing—the story of our brothers' Comrades adventure—and the two of us enjoyed sharing it.

As they had in 2018, the party organizers had Comrades road closure signs to hand out, and Josh and I each got one—and then got them autographed by Fordyce and also by Camille Herron, the 2017 female champion who was also there. Before we left, Josh said that we should get a picture with Fordyce. We went over, and the former champion was gracious as always. Before the picture, he told me I should try again. "You're not heavy, but if you lost a few pounds," was his advice.

Just before someone snapped a picture, Fordyce reached into his pocket and pulled out a huge gold medal. At first, I thought it was some kind of toy. He handed it to me and told me to put it on for the photo. It was heavy, and I examined it closely and turned it over. It was his 1981 Comrades Gold, his first victory. I was blown away and excited to wear it for the picture—a perfect way to finish out the party and the quest for a medal of my own.

CHAPTER 40

Missing the Crazy

My dominant emotion in the months that followed Comrades 2022 continued to be one of peacefulness about how the day had worked out. I was proud that I had tried in 2018, given how far out of my comfort zone the race had been, and that I had come so close to finishing. It also felt good that despite closing in on 60, I had continued to chase my Comrades dream and had not simply accepted my earlier DNF. And, with Josh finishing the race, the day truly felt more like a victory than a defeat.

But despite Fordyce's remark about trying again—Lindsey also thought it was something I might want to keep in the back of my mind—I resolved to accept the loss gracefully and to move on. Trying the race a second time, to my mind, showed persistence and determination, but I felt that trying it a third time, in my 60s, would be fanatic. I knew I could never say that Comrades is completely off the table because I changed my mind before about the race and there is no telling how I might feel about it in a few years. Perhaps like Katherine Switzer, who originally inspired me to try it, I will still be thinking about it at age 70. But, as the months went by, I continued to feel content to put it aside and focus on other goals.

Before my first Comrades, I had given a great deal of thought to what I might want to pursue afterward, regardless of how the race ended. That exercise led me to take on my first 70.3 and, a year later, my first Ironman. I had tried to figure out post-race goals before my second trip to South Africa, but had been unable to commit myself to anything in particular. Part of me wanted to keep ratcheting up the difficulty factor. If I were able to finish Comrades, perhaps I should consider a 100-miler, another out-there distance that I had always thought insane, in much the same way that I had earlier thought about Ironman or even, years before that, the marathon itself. Or, perhaps just a little less crazy, there was a 72-mile race around Lake Tahoe called the "Midnight Express" that looked like it could be interesting. But those races, I concluded, probably only made sense if I had been able to finish Comrades—not in the event of another DNF.

The other idea was one that had been given to me by another runner a few years earlier: to run the six world major marathons—Tokyo, Berlin, London, Chicago, New York and Boston. (Charity entries would be the way to get into races like Boston, where the qualifying standard was going to be impossible for me to meet.) This would be a way to remain focused on the marathon distance while injecting variety and purpose into my race selection. It would also be something that would take years to complete, which I saw as a feature rather than a bug. If the chase for Comrades and Ironman had athletically defined my 50s, perhaps the world majors could be my focus for the decade of my 60s. And, with a 70.3 rotated in every other year or so, I could keep my cross-training focused and goal-oriented.

Josh and I had agreed to spend a few extra days in South Africa after the race. We planned on going on a safari, something neither of us had ever done before. We needed to rent a car for the journey and as I sat in the car rental agency, waiting while Josh handled the paperwork, I scrolled through my emails. By coincidence, I saw that the lottery window had just opened for the Tokyo marathon, and I signed up on the spot, excited about taking my first tentative step toward putting the world majors plan into place. Tokyo is notoriously difficult to get into. Lindsey later told me that another client, also on a quest to complete the world majors, had been trying without success for nine years. To my amazement, a few weeks later I received notification that I had been selected. With that, my quest to run the marathon majors had begun.

For a few months, I continued to stay focused on the majors plan. Ultras and Ironman were now in my past, to become a fading memory. It all made sense as I thought about it, and yet increasingly it didn't feel right. I had really loved being on a journey toward a new and scary goal. In 2011, it had been my first half marathon; in 2012, my first full; in 2018, my first attempt at Comrades; and in 2019, my first Ironman. Each time I had experienced a months-long sense that my life had adventure in it, that there were still new mountains to climb. I missed the crazy.

My first race after Comrades did nothing to dispel my increasing lack of enthusiasm for my new plan. In October, I ran Marine Corps for the third time. I had signed up for it while in South Africa, the day after I had entered the Tokyo lottery. I had hoped to rediscover some of the magic from my first Marine Corps 11 years earlier, and at the same time to reinforce my new focus on the marathon distance. I also wanted to eliminate any residual disappointment from my Comrades DNF and to quickly replace that with a finisher's medal.

In the end, it was a deflating experience. I had hoped to finish in just under five hours which, given the mild weather and flat course profile, seemed straightforward. But after a good first half 13 miles, I began to slow. By mile 19 I had taken a 5-hour finish off the table, and it became a slog. By mile 26, I was doing a run-walk based on landmarks along the side of the course. I didn't want to give up and just walk the remainder. I certainly wasn't panicked or tempted to drop out, but it was unpleasant—other than the second Ironman, by far the worst I had ever felt in the last few miles of a marathon.

As the wheels came off at MCM, I couldn't help but wonder whether I should be rethinking this new focus on marathons. One thing was clear to me. I would not do any more races until my body had sufficiently recovered. In the prior 11 months. I had done an Ironman, a half marathon (for a PR time), a standalone marathon, a marathon with 4.8 miles tacked on to make it a 50 K, 35 miles at Comrades, and then MCM. I had clearly over-extended myself and was wondering whether this had caused my breakdown near the end of Marine Corps. The last race had been my idea, not Lindsey's, and in hindsight it must have been too much too quickly. When I texted Lindsey the day after, he said I should take it easy and not make any decisions until November or December, which made sense to me. At least, I got the medal.

One night in January, I decided to pull up the website for Midnight Express and take a closer look. At 72 miles it was obviously longer than Comrades. But while the race organizers hoped you would finish within 18 hours so that the last 26 miles of your race would overlap with the Lake Tahoe Marathon and its aid stations, it was not a requirement. There would be no intermediate cut-offs to worry about. And while there were some elevation changes, a quick scan of the website suggested that most of this was concentrated in two points on the course, with plenty of flat running in between. There was a matter-of-factness about the whole enterprise that I found appealing: "No whiners or wussies, please! Just get it done. And don't feed the bears!"

I had become convinced through my two Comrades experiences that what made that race so challenging for me was the strict cut-offs. I was not intimidated by the distance. It was the idea of spending all those long hours in an unforgiving race against the clock with very little if any margin for error that I found scary. The fact that Midnight Express was longer didn't deter me, once I took into account a target per-mile pace of 15 minutes for an 18-hour finish, more than two minutes slower than what was required to complete Comrades within 12 hours. And Midnight

Express had one other thing going for it. From watching documentaries and reading race reports over the years, I had become fascinated by the idea of running through the night in nature. It seemed thrilling, perhaps even a little romantic in a strange, running sort of way. Midnight Express, with its 9 p.m. start and scenic route, would give me that opportunity.

Lindsey was enthusiastic about the idea, and I went ahead and signed up, starting myself on yet another endurance adventure. Maybe, I thought, I would always need a little crazy in my life—something to chase, to fire my imagination, to get my blood flowing.

CHAPTER 41

Sorting Things Out

During one of our first sessions after the sign up for Midnight Express, Lindsey told me that on reviewing my training over the prior year, he had become convinced that I did best when I engaged in triathlon rather than traditional ultra-marathon training. Because of that, he was planning on structuring a plan that continued to retain some level of biking and swimming and that limited running to four days per week. My workouts would be light for a month or so, and then we would move into a training block focused on building speed, to be followed by one dedicated to endurance, before tapering for the race. I had complete faith in Lindsey and was determined to follow whatever he had in mind for me. I still worried, after my performance at Marine Corps, that I might be over the hill and incapable of an audacious new challenge like Midnight Express, but I was committed to trying.

After some light training in January, the intensity began to ratchet up. I was feeling pretty good and started to wonder whether I should weave in a 70.3—a legacy of my prior idea of combining the World Majors with a half-Ironman thrown in every other year. I did not think it would be especially challenging, and I liked the idea of keeping my hand in long course triathlons. Lindsey was on board and suggested I target something for May or June. After studying the Ironman website, I could not find one that worked for me in either month. There was, however, a 70.3 in early April in Texas that looked interesting, and I signed up for it. When I told Lindsey about it, he remarked that it was a bit on the early side. Nevertheless, as with Marine Corp a few months earlier, I moved ahead.

My eyes, as it turned out, were bigger than my stomach. It ended up being an awful experience, even worse than Marine Corps. Even though the water wasn't as cold as it had been in Arizona, I experienced some shortness of breath and in general found the swim uncomfortable. The bike started off well enough: straight out for 28 miles with a strong wind at my back. Of course, that meant the second half was directly into the wind and with the added discomfort of rapidly rising temperatures that ultimately reached into the 80s. When I finally got off the bike, I was in no mood to run at all, much less to bang out a half marathon. I started out from transition, assuming that after an uncomfortable mile or two I would be able to find a rhythm and get it done, but I just couldn't get my breathing under control and kept varying my run-walk to try to find something that would settle me. After eight miles of struggle, during which I saw my anticipated finish time get further and further out, I did some math. I had put myself in a position where, to my embarrassment, even being able to finish by the 8:30 cut-off was not a given.

The night before, in my hotel room, I had been reading David Goggins' second book, *Never Finished*. I was at the part where he was describing his first experience running the Moab 240, where a series of mounting physical challenges threatened to force him to drop out. Goggins described the importance of striving to succeed in a race where things have started to go wrong:

> Your willingness to succeed builds self-esteem. It broadens your concept of your own capability, yet it is the first thing we lose touch with when things go bad. After that, giving up often feels like the sanest option, and maybe it is, but know that quitting chips away at your self-worth and always requires some level of mental rehab. . ... A successful mission seldom requires any emotional maintenance (Goggins, 2022).

I thought of Goggins' words as I pondered my next move. I would not quit and believed that there would be value in finishing by the cut-off no matter how ugly—and was equally convinced there would be a lasting impact on my mental toughness if I simply stopped because it was difficult. As I pondered my situation, I realized that if I gave up entirely on trying to find a running rhythm and instead simply walked hard and maintained a 17:30 pace over the last five miles, I would make it with about four minutes to spare. I made the switch and, to my relief, crossed the finish line in time and got my medal. So much for marathons and 70.3s done on barebones training as my new normal. Maybe I really was getting old.

But increasingly, as I thought about Texas, I became convinced that there was another factor at work. I had become sloppy about my weight. In the years since Covid, it had crept up to around 215, and that had clearly hurt me in the Texas heat. I scanned my pictures from the official race photographer and some of them were truly embarrassing. One in particular looked like the "before" picture in a weight loss promotion. I really needed, once and for all, to come up with a nutrition approach that would allow me to get my weight down to a sensible level and to maintain that over the remaining months of training for Midnight Express and, ideally, permanently. I could not continue to train and race at a weight that was above 200 pounds if I was serious about being able to take on a 72-mile ultra or even to run the Majors with any kind of confidence that I could stay injury-free and turn in times that I would feel good about.

Though veganism had done great things for me, one can be a vegan and still overeat. Pizza with vegan cheese is, still, pizza. Simply challenging myself to eat less was not something I could readily translate into action. Reflecting back on my years of experimentation with nutrition before embracing a vegan lifestyle, I racked my brains for a fix or series of fixes that I could internalize as habits, executing them with little or no thought—the hallmark of nearly any successful behavior change.

I experimented for a few weeks and ultimately concluded that success for me would come from a series of smaller tweaks rather than a grand, sweeping change like intermittent fasting, calorie counting, or full abstention from between-meal snacking—all of which I had tried in the past. Eventually, I settled on six main changes which, in one way or another, incorporated the successful elements of the different approaches from my pre-vegan years:

1. Breakfast. There are those who subscribe to the view that breakfast is "the most important meal of the day." Proponents of that approach argue that it should be substantial and calorie rich, but for me, a big breakfast simply meant that I was starting my day having already consumed a significant portion of my allotment of calories, which only put added pressure on my eating choices for later. I decided to go in the opposite direction: a piece of fruit, usually a banana, right after my workout and then a second piece of fruit, usually an apple, as a snack in the mid to late morning. This was inspired by Jesse Itzler (2016) in his book *Living with a Seal:* "only fruit until noon."

2. Lunch. Here I wanted something satisfying while not overdoing it. I found that salmon (a compromise on my veganism that I had introduced a couple of years ago) or a Poke bowl or sushi did the job nicely.

3. Afternoon snacking. As in the morning, I restricted my snacking to fruit, with one exception: at around 5:00, I would have three rice cakes with peanut butter.

4. Dinner. For this meal as well, my goal was to have it be enough to satisfy while not overdoing things. I settled on having one of the same choices that I had considered for

lunch, though not literally the same thing I had eaten earlier in the day. Recalling how night grazing had historically been a nutrition nemesis for me, I resolved that dinner would be on the early side, ideally around 6:00, and there would be no snacking afterward.

5. Alcohol. Over the years, I had become convinced that alcohol in almost any amount is incompatible with maintaining a healthy weight. At various times, I succeeded in cutting alcohol out entirely for a period of months, only to pick it up again. I realized that I needed to limit alcohol to achieve something close to an ideal weight, but that completely abstaining would not work for me. The compromise that I came up with was basically this: no drinking alone.

6. Eating speed. I had read that one key to achieving a desired weight was to slow down the pace of one's eating. Eating too fast, which growing up in a big family had always seemed like a necessity, caused you to continue to eat even after you were full and before your brain received the message that you had eaten enough. That made sense, but how do you slow down your eating? Finally one day, it hit me. I needed to concentrate on taking only a single bite at a time and then fully chewing and then swallowing that entire bite before taking another one. Taking a sip of water between bites would further slow the process down. As someone who tended to wolf down food, I had subconsciously been shoveling in additional forkfuls before I had finished what was already in my mouth. I realized that eating that way was, in addition to being bad for my health, irrational. With a bite of food in my mouth, I was

already enjoying my meal, and adding more did nothing to further alleviate my hunger or increase my satisfaction. In fact, the opposite was true. Eating at high speed made the meal go by faster, inevitably leaving me disappointed and still hungry when it was done. Within only a few days, the new practice felt natural, and I could see that it was allowing me to reach the end of a meal feeling full (or at least fuller), rather than anxious for more.

After a few weeks, the pounds started to come off and kept coming off. By June I was down to 200 and then kept going lower. By August, I had reached 190, and in September the high 180s, before stabilizing in the low 190s. Of course, the real test will be whether I can sustain these changes over the coming years, long after the pressure and motivation from a single upcoming race has passed. As I pondered my successful eating fixes, it occurred to me that Midnight Express had already given me something valuable months before I ever set foot on the course. Anxiety about the immense physical challenge ahead forced me to focus on something that was crucial to my health but that I had previously been willing to ignore, despite the toll it was undoubtedly taking on my long-term wellbeing.

With the drop in weight, my running paces started to improve and, with that, my confidence that perhaps I did still have something left in the tank. The first test was to come in late July. Lindsey wanted to close out the speed block with a half marathon. He thought I could run it in below 2:10, which would be a new PR. Despite my weight loss, I was skeptical. The race I picked out was walking distance from my apartment. The day was going to be hot (70 at the start and climbing to the mid-70s); the race wouldn't begin until 7:30 which would only make the temperature more of a factor; and most of it would be run on a gravel path along a canal, which I assumed would slow my pace. I couldn't help but compare all of this to the New York half from the prior year, where the temperature (in the low 50s at the start) and course surface and profile had all been ideal.

As we gathered for the start, the race director announced that storms the prior afternoon had knocked some trees onto the course. As a result, there were several spots where it would be necessary to climb over fallen trees to continue. Already feeling the pressure to turn in a respectable time under less-than-ideal conditions, this was concerning news. Earlier in the week I had watched a short Goggins Instagram video. It was him, running shirtless as he typically does in these, narrating his second run of the day in more than 100-degree heat: "If life gives you lemons, eat the fucking lemon!" That, I decided, was the attitude I would need for this race.

We crossed the start line, and I dialed into Lindsey's target pace range of between 9:15 and ten minutes per mile, feeling surprisingly good despite the rising temperature and the gravel surface. My plan was to try to stay within the band set by Lindsey for the run intervals, with a slight bias toward the high side. I figured that as it got hotter I would invariably slow down. With that in mind, I wanted to stay on track for as long as possible, which meant not blowing up early from a too-fast start.

Pretty quickly we encountered some downed trees. I moved past them relatively easily, but starting at the 6-mile mark we hit several obstacles that required a complete stop and then queuing up to get through. Adding to the problem was the presence of bicyclists on the course, who had to carry their bikes over the trees, further slowing things down. Except for one particularly awful stretch of trees, I was able to hold the run pace for the entire first half, generally staying in the 9:30s. Reaching the halfway point, I was psyched to turn around and head back. I continued to be able to hold my run pace within the target, around 9:30-9:40, and felt strong—no heavy breathing or leg tightening.

There was one final tree obstacle in the last 100 yards or so, with a cyclist partially blocking the way. I moved to his left to cross without waiting behind him. Surprised, he asked if I was in a hurry, clearly having failed to notice that he was in the middle of a race. "Yes," I told him and kept going.

Almost immediately, I caught sight of the finish. I crossed at 2:13:31, my second fastest half ever. It was not a PR and certainly not the sub-2:10 that Lindsey thought I was capable of, but between the trees, the heat, and the terrain, I was thrilled. And the fact that I felt good all the way through made it even more of a confidence booster. Lindsey was "chuffed" by my performance. It had been precisely what he had hoped for, essentially a return to the speed I had achieved at New York.

The successful half marathon ended the speed block, and we moved into one focused on endurance. This would mean a return to sandwich runs, which we decided would be a longer long run on Sundays and a shorter long run on Mondays. Though I didn't look forward to all those miles, I was excited to get away from the focus on speed. The length of the Sunday long runs ratcheted up over the next six weeks, with the biggest test to come in the second week of September. For that run, Lindsey wanted me to run for six hours. The next day I would need to add another two. Lindsey explained that my pace was not that crucial. These two runs and the other long ones in the coming weeks, including a 5-hour run, would be about "grinding it out."

I had hoped to find a marathon for the 6-hour run but completely struck out. There were a number of seemingly great "flat and fast" options but, as luck would have it, it was the last weekend to qualify for the Boston marathon. Every race that I would have otherwise considered was sold out. Instead, I found a nearby half marathon and constructed a 6-hour run that included a few miles before the race and about two and a half hours of running afterward. It was in the 70s and humid but mercifully cloudy, and I muddled through. I knew the test was only half over, though. I still had to run another two hours the next day, on tired legs, for the weekend to have been a success. I felt surprisingly good the next morning and indeed felt better and got faster as the run progressed—a good sign.

CHAPTER 42

Escape from Burning Man

In late August, with slightly more than six weeks left before Midnight Express, I headed to Nevada to satisfy my end of the Comrades bargain with Josh. He had done his part and then some. Now it was time for me to do mine.

I read up on Burning Man, which had started in 1986 with 35 people on a San Francisco beach and had now grown to more than 70,000 in a remote patch of Nevada desert. Burning Man defied any simple definition. It was one part music festival, one part commune, one part artistic retreat, and one part desert camping trip—all against a backdrop of drug experimentation and sexual innuendo. One writer has described it as the "[w]orld's largest chemically enhanced self-expression festival." (Tower, 2015) Burning Man is famous for its ten principles, which express the ethos and spirit of the event—everything from decommodification (no display of brands), leaving no trace (taking out with you everything, including garbage, that you brought in), radical self-reliance, and radical self-expression. One of the ten principles is "gifting," the giving of things unconditionally, without any expectation of reciprocation. That meant that there would be opportunities to find coffee, snacks, and drinks at various locations during the day, recognizing, of course, that one should be focused on giving as well. There is no exchange of money during Burning Man, with a single exception—you can buy ice.

The radical self-expression manifested itself most notably in the outlandish dress of the participants. From pictures I had seen, it seemed that guys tended either toward something out of Mad Max or wild, mismatched colors. For the women, there were a lot of platform boots and sexy tops. I decided that radical self-expression in clothes, in my case, would be things that I secretly liked but would never be comfortable wearing in public in the non-Burning Man world. I went to several local thrift shops and opted for floral shirts for the day, a doo-rag, beads, a lionhead necklace, a sleeveless jeans vest, and a black leather jacket for the cold nights. I also picked up some practical items for the harsh desert conditions that featured frequent sandstorms; these included a wide brim straw hat, ski goggles, and a dust mask.

I had mixed emotions as Burning Man approached. Had it not been for the deal with Josh, it was something I never would have considered. It featured so many of the things that were not me—dancing and partying in particular—and was raucously social and unfettered in ways that had certainly not characterized my structured, achievement-oriented life. And yet, in a way not entirely unlike how I felt about the ever-increasing physical challenges I had been taking on, I was drawn to the idea of putting myself in a novel, uncomfortable situation that had previously seemed unimaginable.

We reached Burning Man late in the evening in our little caravan of two motorhomes. We showed our tickets and then advanced to the greeter stations. We stepped out of the vehicles and were met by a guy in a plush, head-to-toe animal costume. He asked if there were any first-timers among us, and Josh pointed to me. I was told to lie on the ground and roll around a bit, and then the greeter sprinkled some of the dessert dust on me. After I got back on my feet, he asked for permission to give me a hug (consent is another important Burning Man value) and with it conferred the traditional Burning Man greeting, "Welcome Home!" By the time we got to our site and did some basic organizing, I had been up for 24 hours straight. Josh and the others headed out to enjoy the few remaining hours of darkness, but I had nothing left and decided to defer my real discovery of Burning Man until the morning.

The next day, I walked out of the motor home to a bright sun and cloudless sky and climbed on my bike for a trip out to the "Playa." The Playa is a circular expanse of desert a mile across that sits at the center of the event. Burning Man itself is organized according to a clock design with vertical lanes extending out from the Playa at 15-minute intervals, intersecting with 12 concentric circles of campsites. The "clock" goes from 2:00-10:00, leaving the Playa open along roughly one-third of its perimeter. The "Man" in the Burning Man name refers to a large figure that is mounted on top of an ornate wooden building positioned in the middle of the "Playa." The other structure that is a Burning Man tradition is the "Temple" a few hundred yards away from the Man and positioned at what would be the site's 12:00 spot.

The immensity of Burning Man required reliance on bicycles to get around. After a few minutes of riding, I reached the Playa, and my gaze was immediately drawn to the "Man," rising like a beacon. The Man would be burned during a raucous nighttime ceremony on the second to last day of the event. It was something that I was really looking forward to. I rode toward him, along the way marveling at the outfits and the intricate art installations. Cars are not permitted on the Playa, with the exception of duly registered "mutant vehicles." These were art cars of all shapes and sizes. Over the course of the event, I would see a lighthouse, a cow, several motorboats, a giant telephone, a pirate ship, an elephant, and something that looked like it had come straight out of Mad Max. Traversing the hard, flat surface of the Playa in any direction that caught my fancy and seeing for the first time the Man, the art installations, and mutant vehicles was otherworldly.

I returned to our site, energized by what I had seen. I relayed my impressions to my brother Craig, who had also joined us. Craig and Josh had gone together to Burning Man a few years earlier, and Craig assured me that however remarkable it seemed during the day, the nights were "one hundred times better." That seemed hard to imagine—it had already been so unique—but it made me even more excited about my first night on the Playa.

I was not prepared to ignore my training during my nearly week-long commitment to the Burning Man experience. Swimming was out, of course, but I looked forward to doing my runs on the Playa. I figured that with all the biking that was an inevitable part of the experience, I would be able to check off those boxes as well. After receiving my official greeting the night before by the guy in the full body animal costume, I had also been handed a Reader's Digest-size handbook about the events that would be happening in the various camps. Scheduling an event at one's camp site was a favored way to "gift." I checked the guidebook to see if there was anything running-related. That first afternoon, the guidebook said, there would be a group run at 6:30, originating from the "Run Free" camp. I would do my first Burning Man run with the group.

Attire—or the possible foregoing thereof—was an issue. According to the description in the guidebook: "Run free, with/out clothes on! Meet us at our Pink Dome for a sunset naked run and howl at the end of the day!" Running completely naked was not for me, I concluded—at least, not this early in the experience. I would compromise by going without a shirt, with my flashy necklaces on prominent display, which together with my doo rag was as radical as I was prepared to be. Craig snapped a picture of me checking my phone right before leaving for the run, a perfect "after" picture to balance the awful one from Texas. In the end, I failed to find the group. I had gotten a slow start out of our camp, and they must have left before I got there. I headed out to the Playa by myself, running past the Man and the

Temple and again marveling at the art, vehicles, and wild get-ups that were so uniquely Burning Man.

That first night met the lofty expectations that Josh and Craig had set. To be able to safely experience the Playa at night, it was necessary to light up both your body and your bike. The compound effect in the open space, with everyone similarly illuminated, was stunning. The lights made the people and their bikes stand out while the ground itself remained shrouded in black, which made me feel like I and everyone around me were traveling in space. And beyond, there were colorful lights in every direction—from the various sites along the Esplanade (the innermost ring of the camp), the larger installations along the perimeter of the Playa, the mutant vehicles, and the art. Music echoed from all directions. There were mini concert venues where dozens of revelers were swaying to bass-heavy electric dance music. Sound was also coming from large mutant vehicles that became the center of pop-up dance parties wherever they happened to stop. I stayed out until after three a.m., amazed by it all, until the cumulative exhaustion from the day and chill of the dessert night hit me all at once and finally pushed me to return to our camp.

The next day, a Thursday, was very much a repeat performance. I again toured the Playa by day and, at night, the lights and the sound again mesmerized me. It was perhaps just the tiniest bit of a letdown from the magic of that first day and night when it was all so shocking and new, but marvelous, nonetheless. As we walked during the day, Josh and I talked about the "bet" that had brought him to South Africa and me to the Nevada desert. I had definitely, we both agreed, gotten the better end of it.

I was scheduled for a run on Friday and decided to defer it until later in the day, around sunset, the same time as my Wednesday run. Though the Playa itself is utterly flat, the area is surrounded in all directions by mountains, which made for a dazzling sunset as the sun disappeared behind a nearby peak. That time of the day had its own devotees, which created a nice vibe as Burning Man transitioned between its daytime and nighttime incarnations.

Clouds began to move in during the afternoon and, with them, the first drops of an unexpected desert rain. At first, it was just a minor annoyance. With our RVs and the two shelters that we had constructed on our site, there was no great difficulty in keeping dry and comfortable. That wasn't the case for a couple who was staying right next to us in a tent. They came over, told us they were not set up for these conditions, and then, after giving us a bunch of their supplies, packed up and left. I was amazed that anyone, having come all the way out here, would cut their adventure short. Within a few hours, though, it became clear that they had shown remarkable foresight.

The rain picked up, and the ground became a muddy, unnavigable mess. We learned that the organizers had shut down the entrances; no one could get in or out. That was a big step. Friday is normally a popular arrival day, right before the burning of the Man on Saturday night and the temple on Sunday night. There was also a "shelter in place" order confining all of us to our campsites, which meant there would be no Playa adventure that night. In my case, it also meant the cancelation of my Friday run.

We woke on Saturday to an altered reality. The rain had stopped, but few people were moving around. The desert mud had a way of caking on your shoes so that almost immediately it was as though you were walking with cinder blocks on your feet. By the afternoon, things had sufficiently dried out that I was able to make it out to the Playa on foot. It was still too muddy for bikes. As I passed by other camps, I noticed several where folks were already beginning to take down the various themed displays they had created, reflecting that the mood had changed. Burning Man wasn't over, but it wasn't itself, either.

It wasn't clear when the gates would be opened to permit people to leave. Each year, the departure for the those who decided to stay until the last day—the "Exodus" in Burning Man parlance—was brutal. The year before, cars had waited in line for eight hours before finally getting out. We had hoped to miss that by leaving on Sunday morning, the day before the traditional Exodus. The rain had taken away our ability to sneak out early, with official word that the earliest that cars would be permitted to leave would be Monday.

Though cars would not be permitted to leave on Sunday, we learned that the "Burner buses" would be departing that day as scheduled. These traveled between the festival and either Reno or San Francisco, and you needed to have purchased your ticket in advance. Craig had always planned on taking the bus, and I walked him over to the official gathering point for the lucky ticket holders. There the organizers announced that the buses couldn't come onto the property because of the mud and that it would be necessary for bus passengers to walk out to the road and be picked up there. It looked to be a 2-3 mile walk.

I decided to walk Craig out, and we continued for a while, until reaching a temporary fence marking the edge of Burning Man territory. I turned around there and resolved that I would leave the next day, following the same path that Craig had taken. (Josh, together with Michael, the fourth member of our group, were planning on driving the motor homes out later in the week, when the departure would be more civilized.) I saw an official announcement on the Burning Man website a few hours later which advised attendees that they could do just that and that on the road they would be met by a shuttle that would take them to a nearby town, from which they would catch a bus to Reno. Since Reno was the city I would be flying out of, that sounded great to me. When I woke up Monday morning, I saw that the website had been updated. The good news was that cars would be permitted to start driving out, though an Exodus nightmare clearly awaited those who decided to leave immediately rather than wait one day or, more likely two or three, for the departing crowds to thin out. The bad news was that the roadside shuttle service had been canceled, and we were being advised not to walk out.

I decided that I was going to leave, shuttles or not. I knew I wouldn't be stopped. Radical self-reliance and self-expression do have benefits. But I also decided that the route Craig had taken would not work for me. Leaving Burning Man only to end up on the side of a road with random cars passing by did not sound like a promising plan for getting a ride to Reno. Instead, I would walk out along the line of exiting cars. Then, when I reached the front, I would turn around, hold up a sign with "Reno" written on it, and hope that a departing Burner, still feeling the gifting vibe, would pick me up.

I helped Josh and Michael break down the camp. After five hours of that, I showered and headed out, wearing a backpack, pulling a roller bag, and carrying a Reno sign that Josh had painted for me. Soon enough, I reached the back of the line of waiting vehicles—actually, eight lines. I walked between two of the lanes - surrounded by stationary recreational vehicles that towered above me. There wasn't a cloud in the sky, and the temperature was starting to climb. I started to get nervous about the heat. I had put on jeans for the flight—not the best choice for a desert walk that was stretching into its second hour. As I progressed, I kept thinking that I had to be getting close. Yet, the actual exit was nowhere in sight. Periodically, I would call up to someone sitting in a chair on top of a motorhome to ask if they could see the exit. Each time the answer I got was "no," and I continued on.

Finally, after two and a half hours of walking, I could see where the eight lanes combined into two and from there into one. This was my moment. Going all the way to the front would mean asking someone who was finally about to reach the highway after eight hours in line to stop one more time—and that would be too much. About a hundred yards short of the end, I turned around, held up my sign, and waited. Within ten minutes I had my ride and with it, a hot, dusty, memorable exit from Burning Man. The training schedule had called for a 2-hour run that day, which had been out of the question. But, I decided, my nearly 8-mile trek through the desert, lugging bags, had been a good substitute.

CHAPTER 43

Midnight Express

Back from Burning Man, I resumed training. My long runs were going well—not just knocking out the miles but also hitting the pace targets that Lindsey set for me, despite the heat and humidity of what continued to be a very hot summer. My running stride felt comfortable and my energy level high. It was a return to the "Superman" feeling that the last stages of Ironman training had given me, and a wonderful reward for having taken on this challenge.

Wanting to leave as little as possible to chance, I headed out six days early for the race, to acclimate to Lake Tahoe's 6,224 feet altitude. On Thursday, with only two days to go, the race director held a Zoom orientation. During the call, I learned there actually *are* bears out there. I had thought the reference on the website to not feeding the bears was just a joke. The director assured us, however, that they are not dangerous. They might charge toward you and pretend to attack, but they would not actually do that. They just wanted food. Of course, I would be running with a backpack loaded with gels and snacks, which certainly seemed like food to me, but if the organizers weren't worried about it, I decided, I shouldn't be either.

The website had instructed us to provide our own support for the first 48 miles of the race. For the final 24 miles, assuming you were on track for an 18-hour finish, you could use the aid stations on the Lake Tahoe Marathon, which would be run Sunday morning. Otherwise, you would need to provide your own support for that part of the race as well. It was going to be a lot to ask of anyone—to come all the way out to Nevada and spend an entire night and potentially most of the next day driving around the lake and periodically meeting up with me so that I could replenish my nutrition.

I thought carefully about whom to ask and then realized who would be perfect: Jason Schwartz. He was the guy who had started me on this fitness journey 13 years earlier. Jason was an accomplished ultra-runner in his own right, having completed two 50-milers, and he understood what races like Midnight Express were all about. He was also the very epitome of positivity, which would be hugely helpful during the long hours of racing when, invariably, my spirits would flag. I reached out and, to my immense relief, Jason agreed immediately.

The looming mental challenge became my preoccupation during those final days, as I had little to do other than hang out and get used to the altitude. My fitness was great, my weight was exactly where I wanted it to be, and I had stayed injury free despite the plantar nightmare from the year before. But I wondered how I would deal with the mental part, to not get overwhelmed by the anticipation of the long hours of running through the night, followed by ten or more additional hours of effort once the sun rose. What if I began to really feel physical distress? Would I be able to rally myself to continue despite the discomfort? The only thing that could defeat me in this race, I concluded, would be an exhausted version of me, convincing myself that a successful finish was impossible and that I had no choice but to drop out.

On the Thursday before the race, I had my final session with Lindsey. He took me through the strategy that he wanted me to follow. He told me that I should target a finish of between 17 and 18 hours. This would be based on a six minute/one minute run/walk strategy, with the run intervals in the 12:30-13:00 MPM pace, for an overall pace closer to 14:00 MPM. He also called out six spots on the course where there were significant hills of more than a mile in length. He suggested that I walk a majority of these sections. I jotted down the locations so that I could take them with me on the course and make sure I was identifying them correctly. He summed up by telling me that this was the best prepared I had ever been since the two of us started working together and that he looked forward to seeing how I would do.

Satisfied with the practical guidance, I asked Lindsey if he had any suggestions for the mental part. He immediately rattled off several ideas, all thoughtful and practical. He told me that if I felt that I needed it, a 20-minute nap could be immensely restorative. If I were to do it, he cautioned, I would be stiff immediately upon waking and would need to start slowly until my body warmed back up. Later in the race, as I became more tired, I might find it valuable to give myself rewards for reaching a particular landmark or running for some amount of time. The reward could be a special treat, a walk, or even a sitting break. It was key, he explained, to make sure to get to mile 60. From there, I would know that I could finish no matter what. Finally, he told me to regularly remind myself, "I'm fit; I'm strong; I can keep going."

The day before the race I made my final purchases. I picked up some bins for my various race day supplies: water and Gatorade bottles, gels, protein bars, a change of shoes, extra salt tablets, a first aid kit, and other odds and ends. As I shopped, I thought of Lindsey's suggestion that I might want to reward myself with treats late in the race. I had read an article a few weeks earlier in an ultra-running magazine about using Pay Day candy bars as a race snack. The author argued that the calorie count was about right and, most important, they were delicious. The same could not be said of gels, hours into a long race. I picked up a package of Pay Days and decided to supplement my treat supply with two other candies that I really loved but almost never allowed myself to eat: Lindor's Truffles and Ghirardelli chocolates filled with caramel.

Jason and I met up the morning before the race. He was upbeat as always and, at the same time, focused on the practical aspects of the challenge ahead. At his suggestion, we headed out to drive the course. The route called for several turns and, because the roads would not be closed and the course would be unmarked, there was a real danger of making a mistake. Indeed, twice during the drive we missed turns, each time backtracking and approaching a second time to make sure that we identified the spot correctly.

The drive was eye-opening for a reason that went beyond navigation. For the first time, I realized how superficial my review of the course topography had been on the race website. I had thought that the course had two sections with climbing but was, otherwise, essentially flat, an enlarged version of the benign Trap Pond 50K course with its pine-needle-covered forest trail. Instead, it had a very Comrades-like profile—constant ups and downs and virtually no flat sections along the entire 72-mile route. A closer inspection of the website, following the drive, alerted me that there were 4,800 feet of climbing, which meant, since it was a loop course that finished where it started, an equal amount of descending. This was almost as much vertical as Comrades. If I had paid better attention before signing up, I might have decided to pick a different race, but it was too late now. I hoped that my fitness would be enough to carry me through.

On Saturday, I stayed in bed nearly the whole day with my feet up and, as the sky began to darken, felt fully rested. In those last hours, I wasn't anxious about the race, unlike with Ironman or Comrades. If anything, my dominant emotion was one of impatience. As evening fell, I went through my final preparations, and then Jason and I headed to the hotel parking lot where the participants were gathering, the start of the race only a few minutes away.

CHAPTER 44

41 Down/31 to Go

About 20 of us were waiting in front of the hotel. A few minutes after I joined the group, the race organizer called out the start in a casual voice, and we were off. The temperature was in the low 50s, and I started in shorts, arm warmers, and no gloves. We settled into a rhythm as we moved down the street, initially staying on a sidewalk before having to switch to a shoulder. One other thing I had noticed on the drive was that there were very few bike paths or sidewalks along the course, and the shoulders were often not wide at all, sometimes nearly up against a guardrail. That was going to make for a bit of stress, especially for the Saturday night portion during which, as the race organizer warned us in the Thursday Zoom call, we could expect drunk drivers on the road. I was particularly concerned about a tunnel some ten miles in, where it was going to be incredibly tight. The organizer had told us that if we wanted, we could be driven through the tunnel, though in the end I had not thought to ask Jason to meet me there.

Those first miles were a pleasure, the running effortless. I had done my final four-hour long run entirely at night and it seemed natural now to be running in the dark. The "view" as well was compelling. The Tahoe area experiences little light pollution, and the night was cloudless, which made for a brilliant, star-filled sky. Then, up ahead, I saw the tunnel. It was relatively short, perhaps 30 or 40 yards, and I approached it cautiously. A small ledge about 6 inches wide ran through about half of it, and I walked on that. After the ledge, the space really tightened. I started to sprint the final distance but caught sight of a car coming, turned around, and stepped back on the ledge. After it passed, I again checked for cars, didn't see another one, and darted through the rest of the tunnel, relieved to have it behind me.

Jason and I had worked out that we would meet every nine miles. I hoped to cover that distance in roughly two hours and had decided to divide the race into eight or nine of these "chunks." My shorter long run each week had usually been 2 hours and 20 minutes, a distance that had come to feel routine, which made the case for 2-hour chunks especially compelling. At the first stop, I grabbed a pair of gloves. Starting without them had been a mistake. My hands were stiff and barely able to function, and Jason, seeing my condition, quickly took over the refilling of my bottles. We agreed to meet again in another nine miles. We repeated the cycle two more times, grabbing more gels and snacks, Jason refilling my bottles, and then back at it. I was not at all bothered by running in the darkness. If anything, after a summer of training in heat and humidity, I relished being away from the sun.

During the fourth cycle, it started again. The left knee that had inexplicably given me so much trouble at Comrades began to hurt. Just like the last time, the pain kept increasing until it was impossible to ignore. My pace dropped, and the well-crafted plan to think only about the current 2-hour "chunk" fell apart. With at least ten more hours still ahead and likely more given the drop off in my speed, it was impossible to see how I could pull off finishing the race with this amount of pain. The fact that it was the same knee as in South Africa made me think that there must be a structural problem that had never been diagnosed—some type of weakness that was only exposed in race conditions with a significant amount of downhill.

I decided to try a couple of things to get it under some semblance of control. At the next stop, I would take some Advil and then get into the passenger seat of the car for the 20-minute nap that Lindsey had suggested, hoping that while I slept the painkillers might begin to work. Upon waking, I would radically change my run/walk—from 6/1 to 1/2. I thought this would put a lot less pressure on the knee. At the same time, recalling my Ironman marathon splits, I thought I could maintain a sub-15:00 minute per mile pace even with this amount of walking.

I fully reclined the passenger seat and closed my eyes, managing to sleep for most of the 20 minutes. Jason woke me, and I got out of the car, pulled on my backpack, and headed back out. The car had been parked at the base of a steep climb and, as I walked up it, I was dismayed to discover that the pain in the left knee was even worse. Every step was uncomfortable, and in my mind the conversation immediately picked up from where it had left off before the nap. Doing this for ten more hours was not going to be possible. So, that would be it. I would call Jason, tell him my race was over, and he would drive me back to the hotel. Relief washed over me.

But then I thought about having to explain it to everyone who knew I was out here doing this race. After visualizing the sharing of the news of my latest failure, the idea of quitting lost its luster. Perhaps the knee was hurting so much right after the nap because of the stiffness that Lindsey had warned about. I resolved to defer thoughts of quitting. There was no reason to rush to get out of the race. I needed to warm up and give the new 1-minute/2-minute ratio a chance to calm the knee. I got to the top of the hill and started back up.

After a few cycles, the pain in the left knee began to subside. It still hurt but not at a level that felt unsustainable. I wasn't yet committed to trying to finish but began to set intermediate goals. It would be great, I thought, to at least go farther than the 35 miles I had covered at my second Comrades. It would be even better to do more than the 56 miles Josh had run during his Comrades finish. Even between brothers separated by nearly 20 years, there is still something to be said for family bragging rights. Though I usually tried to avoid thinking ahead to the ground still to cover in a long race, this time it was serving me, taking me from a focus on my immediate discomfort to the excitement of what seemed to be achievable targets. From time to time, I would repeat Lindsey's mantra: "I'm fit; I'm strong; I can keep going." I also reminded myself of the slogan I had seen so many times on signs at marathons: "Pain is temporary, victory is forever." I wasn't yet sold on finishing, but I knew that if I could somehow pull it together and stay out there, I would have an accomplishment that I would cherish for the rest of my life. By mile 41, something had clicked. It would be uncomfortable and slow, but I would do it. I pulled out my phone and sent a text to my kids: "41 down/31 to go."

For the next nine miles I stayed on track. The left knee adjusted nicely to the new cadence, and the pain had stabilized at a manageable level. The sun was out and, much as I had liked the night running, the transition to daylight was a mood elevator. My energy remained high, and Jason always commented on the big smile that I wore each time I approached the car. And all those candies were really helping.

As I got closer to 50 miles, I pulled out my slip of paper with Lindsey's hill callouts. Three significant hills stood between miles 50 and 59. I told myself that given Lindsey's instruction to walk most of these, they would be a break for me. The first one, starting right at mile 50 and continuing for nearly three miles, promised to be the worst. By the time I reached the third and final hill, the bottoms of my feet were in full protest. It felt as though they had been clenched for hours, gripping the road as I climbed.

I reached the 60-mile mark that Lindsey had told me to aim for but knew that at my slow pace—I was barely running at this point—I still had three or four hours left until the finish. I kept moving, my concerns now also including my electronics as my Garmin died and the battery life on my phone dropped to single digits, leaving me with only an inexpensive Timex to at least track the time. I sent Jason a text that my phone was about to die. A short while later, he pulled onto a side street right ahead of where I was. He had already scouted this part of the course and showed me an arrow that turned us onto the side street. He also pointed to another arrow farther ahead that indicated another turn. Soon I was in a neighborhood, my feet aching and my energy sinking. More arrows took me through an ever more circuitous path, with each turn worsening my mood. Then, I came upon a giant chalk-scrawled sign on the road surface: 6.2 miles to go. That was depressing. I had estimated that I was within three or, at the most, four miles of finishing. If my walking pace had fallen to 20 minutes per mile—a possibility that I had to consider—that would mean two more hours of this.

I had been guzzling fluids as the day had warmed, hoping to ward off dehydration, and I desperately needed to pee. There was nothing to do about it in a residential neighborhood, no discrete peeing behind a tree in this portion of the course. Eventually, we were out of the neighborhood and into what looked like a small nature preserve, where I found a porta potty on the side of the path. After finishing, I turned to unlock the door, but in just the few moments I had been standing, my legs had completely stiffened. I exited clumsily and made a mental note: no more stopping for any reason. I kept moving forward, my pace still slowing, my foot discomfort getting worse. I had a new fear. What if I tripped and fell? If that happened, I could expect everything to seize up and, with that, my race would be over, whether I wanted to continue or not.

I hadn't seen Jason in hours—not since he had alerted me to the first arrow—and then suddenly there he was again, pulling up ahead of me. He showed me where to turn left and told me to go to the end of the street and then turn right and the finish line would be right there. I was relieved. Less than a mile to go now. I continued to move, Frankenstein-like, every step feeling like a minor victory. I got to the end and turned. Off in the distance, I saw a group of four people standing next to an orange cone. The finish line, in all its understated glory.

I walked across, acknowledging the accomplishment but not really feeling anything. I received my finisher's medal and hugged Jason. After 20 hours and 40 minutes of effort, I had made it.

CHAPTER 45

Find Your Ironman...
And Your Comrades

As always after big races, I considered what the experience had meant to me and, equally important, what it meant for my future racing plans. I was proud to have finished. It had been at the outer limits of my capabilities, and yet I had managed it. If nothing else, it solidified my sense of myself as an ultra-runner and, no less important, as someone who didn't quit when things got tough. I was also pleased to discover that I had come in 5th out of 7 finishers, less than 7 minutes behind the third and fourth place runners who had crossed together and over four hours ahead of 6th place. And, at age 61, I had been the oldest of the group.

I had no desire to look for ways to further one-up myself. Comrades was off the table. While 12 hours of running might seem like less to bite off after nearly 21 hours of effort, I felt that the much faster pace required for a successful finish in South Africa ruled it out once and for all. Going even farther—tackling 100 miles—just had no appeal for me.

In many ways my fitness journey until Midnight Express had been linear or, more accurately, along two parallel paths. With running, I had increased steadily from the 10K distance all the way to 72 miles. With triathlon, I had gone from a sprint to a full Ironman. Now, I decided, I needed to broaden my vision. There are a nearly infinite variety of fitness challenges and experiences, including, to name but a few, 50K and 50 mile trail ultras; the Goggins Challenge (running 4 miles every 4 hours for 48 hours); long hikes like the Grand Canyon rim to rim; multi-day bike tours; and ocean swims. And the World Majors are still a goal for my 60s, a way to stay committed to the marathon distance. The time has come to open my mind to all the options. There will always need to be an element of challenge, enough to keep me focused on 6-day-a-week training and the maintenance of a healthy weight. No doubt every few years I will miss the crazy—the sense that I am on a journey toward something special and a bit scary—and once again take on something outside my comfort zone.

As I look back over my running and triathlon journey for the prior 12 years, Ironman and Comrades loom largest. They represent two seemingly contradictory ideas. Ironman is the embodiment of its motto that "anything is possible," that through strenuous effort you can achieve something that at one point in your life could not have been imagined. Comrades, for its part, represents the hard truth that not *everything* is possible. You can put in the work but still, on race day, come up short. But you don't truly know what you are capable of unless you try, and that narrow, BHAG-like space between what is at the outer reach of possible and what is just beyond is to be sought rather than avoided. As Norman Vincent Peale once said, "Shoot for the moon. Even if you miss, you'll land among the stars." (Goodreads, 2025) I became an Ironman and later a Midnight Express finisher *because* I tried Comrades. Neither would have happened otherwise.

I think a strong argument can be made that you should continue to seek your limits, which you can only really identify by coming up short in the pursuit of a lofty goal. If all you have at the end of the day is an unbroken string of successes, there actually is an element of failure in that—an unwillingness to push the envelope, to take chances, to risk defeat. No endurance athlete wants to see a DNF on their official race result, but as the old runner's adage goes: "A DNF is greater than a DNS [did not start]." Or, as Michelangelo is reported to have said: "The greatest danger for most of us is not that our aim is too high, and we miss it but that it is too low, and we reach it." (Robinson, 2009). I think the secret is to find your Ironman—and your Comrades. Find that challenge that pushes you almost beyond your capabilities and surprise yourself with what you can actually do, which for me ended up being my two Ironman finishes, the second at age 59, followed by Midnight Express at age 61. And then, probe further and see if even more might be possible. Don't be afraid to come up short. There will be growth regardless of the outcome.

The benefits, along the way, are immense. We are living through a period of intense interest in "longevity," the idea that we can extend the length of our lives through a variety of lifestyle and medical interventions. I agree, though, with

Dr. Peter Attia, author of the mammoth bestseller *Outlive*, who argues that our main focus should be on increasing "healthspan" (the portion of life in which we are fit and healthy). To accomplish this, Attia places primary emphasis on the benefits of regular exercise, contending that even if he was certain that it would reduce lifespan by a year, he would still recommend it to his patients for the immense, decades-long improvement in life quality that it can provide. It has certainly worked for me. Endurance sports have injected vitality and adventure into the decade of my 50s and have kicked off my 60s with the promise of more to come.

All this fitness activity and self-challenging are not only about physical well-being, however. My professional life and my personal development outside of fitness are more important to me than what I can accomplish in races. Yet, I don't regard the three spheres of my life as being in competition with one another. I see them instead as mutually supportive, like three separate strands wound together to form a single length of rope that is stronger than any individual strand. In some respects, the working of the various strands together is obvious. The science is clear, for example, that physical activity improves mental health and cognitive function, making me a more positive and optimistic partner and parent and helping extend my professional runway. More prosaically, it is often during a run that I do my best thinking about a particular personal or work challenge.

I think, though, it goes beyond that. The willingness to take on challenges, including ones that demand an extended commitment of time and effort, is something I have tried to cultivate in all areas of my life, not just fitness. The same motivation that has driven me to Ironman and ultras has also helped me through my unusual academic journey, my quest to become a writer, my transition from a staid law practice to the exciting world of corporate start-ups—and most important of all, the partnering in the raising of four wonderful children who continue to delight. I have found that the relationship between my fitness and my personal and professional lives is reciprocal. Sometimes, a previous accomplishment in my personal life gives me confidence that I can take on a scary fitness or professional goal, and other times the inspiration flows outward following the accomplishment of an endurance challenge. As one ultrarunner put it in a recent documentary: "Life makes you a better ultra-runner and then ultra-running makes you better at life." (Brackley, 2020)

I believe the competing Ironman and Comrades ideas are great metaphors for life. Sometimes, with the right amount of effort and discipline, we can achieve things we once thought impossible—like the launch of a new business or the successful management of a major health struggle. Other times, we will fall short, perhaps having a marriage fail or getting fired from a job that we loved. Successes and failures create challenges for us; we need to stay grounded and continue to move forward regardless of outcome. Success should never lead to complacency or over-confidence; there will always be new mountains to climb. We also want to ensure that our failures do not define us and that we are able to find a way to continue despite a setback. Endurance racing is an ideal way to create challenging experiences in a controlled environment—to encounter success and failure and along the way develop those perseverance and optimism qualities that will serve us in all spheres of our lives.

And now, at the start of my seventh decade and after more than 13 years of endurance adventures that include successes I never thought possible, I find myself at a crossroads. I have stopped planning, beyond the World Majors. Instead, I will let my body and my desires at the time decide for me. What I know, though, is this: I want to always live a life of challenge and audacity in everything that I do. Eventually, age and presumably illness will take their toll and I will no doubt be forced to cede ground, but I will do so only reluctantly and hopefully with dignity. I will give age its due but not embrace it as an excuse to coast. Anything, or, more realistically, *almost* anything, is possible. Indeed, even the unlikeliest among us can become an Ironman.

References

Attia, P. (2023). *Outlive*. Harmony.

Brackley, R. (2020). "The Ultra Mindset." Endurance Sports TV.

Collins, J. (2001). *Good to Great*. Harper Business.

Comradesmarathon. (2022). Instagram. https://www.instagram.com/p/Caz2gOtoROR/.

Crowley, C. , & Lodge, H. S. (2007). *Younger next year: Live strong, fit, and sexy—until you're 80 and beyond*. Workman Publishing Company.

Fink, D., & Fink, M. (2004). *Be Iron Fit*. Lyons Press.

Fink, D. & Fink, M. (2014). *IronFit Secrets for Half Iron-Distance Triathlon Success*. Lyons Press.

Galloway, J. (2002). *Galloway's Book on Running*. Shelter Publications.

Goggins, D. (2022). *Never finished: Unshackle your mind and win the war within*. Lioncrest Publishing.

Itzler, J. (2016). *Living with a seal: 31 days training with the toughest man on the planet.* Center Street.

Peale, N.V. (2025). Norman Vincent Peal Quotes. Goodreads. https://www.goodreads.com/author/quotes/8435.Norman_Vincent_Peale.

Robinson, K. (2009). *The Element: How Finding Your Passion Changes Everything.* Penguin Books.

Roosevelt, E. (2016) Eleanor Roosevelt. National Archives: Franklin D. Roosevelt Presidential Library and Museum. Downloaded from https://www.fdrlibrary.org/eleanor-roosevelt.

Steinberg, J. (2011). *You are an Ironman: How Six Weekend Warriors Chased Their Dream of Finishing the World's Toughest Triathlon.* Viking.

Super Marathon/Half Marathon. (2024). https://www.super-marathon.com.

The 72 Mile Tahoe MidnightExpress. (2021). https://www.laketahoemarathon.com/midnight-express.

Thompson, H. S. (1998). *The Proud Highway: Saga of a Desperate Southern Gentleman, 1955-1967.* Ballantine Books.

Tower, Wells. (2015). "The Old Man at Burning Man." GQ. https://www.gq.com/story/burning-man-experiences-wells-tower.

Trason, Ann. *AZQuotes.com*. https://www.azquotes.com/quote/588639.

Yang, B. (2018). *The Why: Running 100 Miles*. https://www.youtube.com/watch?v=8YWyac1ZdsU.

1. During my bodybuilding days, around 1985.

2. Marine Corps Marathon, on the way to a personal best, 2014.

RACING AGAINST TIME | 305

3. Philadelphia Marathon, no more mountains to climb, 2016

4. With Bruce Fordyce, Comrades 2018.

5. At Arthur's Seat, Comrades 2018.

6. Comrades, 2018.

7. Valley of a Thousand Hills, Comrades, 2018.

Cut-off-Points				
Point	Plan	Cut Off	Time	To Go
Lion Park N3	2:10	2:30	8:00	75
Cato Ridge	4:04	4:20	9:50	60
Drummond (half)	5:48	6:10	11:40	46
Winston Park	7:36	8:00	13:30	33

8. My laminated card with the cut-offs, Comrades 2018

9. The Stadium, Comrades 2018

10. My Garmin display, Comrades 2018.

RACING AGAINST TIME | 309

11. With the autographed road closure sign at the post-race party, Comrades 2018.

12. Finishing my first 70.3, Atlantic City, 2018.

13. Atlantic City 70.3, riding in the rain, 2019.

14. About to start the race, Ironman Arizona 2019.

15. Beginning the bike leg, Ironman Arizona 2019.

16. Orlie's Poster, Ironman Arizona 2019.

17. Ironman Arizona, arms raised at the finish,
still wearing the hoodie, 2019

18. The start of the Los Angeles Marathon,
the last big city marathon prior to the Covid closures.

RACING AGAINST TIME | 313

19. Los Angeles Marathon, turning in a Comrades qualifying time, 2020.

20. Maine 70.3, exiting the water after a bad swim, 2021.

21. Main 70.3, struggling on the bike, 2021.

22. Getting my bike fit sorted out after Maine 70.3, 2021.

23. Just before the start of the swim, Ironman Arizona 2021.

24. Finishing, Ironman Arizona 2021.

25. With Orlie after the finish,
my face showing the strain, Ironman Arizona 2021.

26. New York City Half Marathon,
on the way to a new personal best, 2022.

27. San Francisco Marathon (note Alcatraz in the background), just before the plantar returns, 2022.

28. With Josh with the start line in view, Comrades 2022

29. Josh and I running side by side, Comrades 2022.

30. Josh and I as the wheels come off, Comrades 2022.

31. After Comrades 2022 with Josh,
Lindsey Parry in the middle, and Trevor on the far left

32. Comrades 2022 after party with Bruce Fordyce,
wearing Bruce's first gold medal.

33. Marine Corps Marathon, running out of gas, 2022.

34. Texas 70.3, April 2023, the "before" picture.

35. Burning Man, August 2023.

36. Burning Man, August 2023, the "after" picture.

37. The view across Lake Tahoe during Midnight Express, October 2023

38. The last few steps, Midnight Express, October 2023.

39. With Jason after the finish, Midnight Express, October 2023.

www.ingramcontent.com/pod-product-compliance
Lightning Source LLC
Chambersburg PA
CBHW050125170426
43197CB00011B/1717